PRAISE FOR *365 ALIVE!*

"The first time I heard the term 'story activist' was when I discovered the work of Mary Alice Arthur. Her work in the world embodies that activism. While we all know that story is powerful, this book empowers the reader to truly be a story activist in their own lives — and in the process, story the world into a better place. I love how it is easy to dip into this book, learn something new about story and then be offered actionable ways to take that knowledge back into my own life. Wherever you are in the field of story, you will discover something new."
Cate Friesen, TheStorySource.ca (Canada)

"*365 ALIVE!* invites you into an adventure by discovering stories that matter to you. This beautiful book is a trail guide to making stories your allies. Mary Alice Arthur provisions you for a year-long journey with great questions, challenges, and insights for an expedition to know yourself, know your world, and how to navigate with curiosity and grace."
Peggy Holman, author of *Engaging Emergence: Turning Upheaval into Opportunity*, co-author, *The Change Handbook*, co-founder of Journalism That Matters (USA)

"Simple, deep, and inviting, *365 ALIVE!* is a gift of wisdom and a spark of inspiration for a world in urgent need of both. Mary Alice guides us on a journey to unearth the stories that influence who we are individually and collectively. She offers a treasure chest of prompts to surface how story influences the ways we live, and she calls us up to choose the stories that will carry us forward. Anyone seeking to make sense of life in a discombobulating world will find a creative path in *365 ALIVE!*"
Wendy C. Morris, Founder and Principal Consultant, Creative Leadership Studio (USA)

"In *365 ALIVE!* Mary Alice Arthur is your coach taking you on a guided meditation over fifty-two glorious weeks, immersing you in your stories. By the end you know yourself in a new way and appreciate the stories that flow through and around you. Mary Alice's global experience, nuanced understanding of all things narrative, and her beautiful stories take you deep into your own experience, resulting in a meaningful and delightful adventure."
Shawn Callahan, author of *Putting Stories to Work: Mastering Business Storytelling* (Australia)

"A brilliant guide to help surface our stories, befriend them, and toss them around, so we might tap into their power and potential. Stories are elemental to our personal leadership, and to address the complexities we face."
Samantha Slade, author of *Going Horizontal* (Canada)

"Mary Alice's book reminds us all of the important role that stories play in our lives — how they can help shape, build and form everything from how we think to what we see and feel. She digs deep into the therapeutic role our personal stories can play in both evaluating our past and envisioning our future. Her use of provocative questions and reflections at the end of each "chapter" really kickstarts your storytelling possibilities! A wonderful read whether weekly or just straight through and a great reminder for everyone of the power and significance of the stories they carry."
Shane Meeker, author of *StoryMythos: A Movie Guide to Better Business Stories* (USA)

"Mary Alice shows you how to translate your love for storytelling into a mindfulness practice that not only improves your storytelling skills, it improves your peace of mind, relationships and ability to influence others."
Annette Simmons, author of *The Story Factor* (USA)

"I've been teaching storytelling for over 30 years now and wish that I had Mary Alice Arthur's *365 ALIVE!* for every one of those classes. This is a book on storytelling that manages to be both an intimate consideration of what story is and does and a practical approach to the how and why of making meaningful stories. Whether you use it as a fifty-two-week journey or a compendium of why storytelling matters, this one deserves to be in your essential storytelling library."

Loren Niemi, storyteller and author of *Inviting the Wolf In: Thinking About Difficult Stories*, with Elizabeth Ellis (USA)

"In *365 ALIVE!* every day becomes a new way to look at and engage with story. The stories around you, the stories you tell, the stories others tell, and the stories not yet told. Finally…a guide that allows for creative, inclusive, and multi-dimensional strategies and tools to get after and get into 'story' and bring the many stories alive that are transforming our world."

Christine Chopyak, author of *Picture Your Business Strategy: Transform Decisions with the Power of Visuals* (USA)

"In this unique time on our planet we are sensing that we are all interconnected, much more than we imagined, and that we have a chance now to reflect — What story are we a part of? Do we want to repeat our past story? Or is it time to live a new, bold story that can continue to grow as we grow, day by day? Through her own life, Mary Alice is not only walking the talk, but she has now written a book that invites us to create the story we want to tell with our lives, day by day. *365 ALIVE!* has my warmest recommendations."

Peter Engberg, film director, explorer and speaker (Denmark)

"A unique book full of exquisitely wrought and extraordinarily powerful questions, guiding you on a journey into your own life stories and back out into the world again. Mary Alice's wise, provocative and generous counsel is the companion you need if you long to be helpful in this critical moment in our world but are not sure how."

Jenny Blagdon, social innovator, educator, coach (Australia)

"This is a masterful work in using stories for your personal development and growth. Many people talk about using stories in this way, but few actually give you concrete steps to do it. This is the only book I've come across that offers new ways to think about, discover, and use your stories so thoroughly. You will come out of the experience transformed. Grab it today. The time you put into this exploration will pay dividends for life."

Dr. Karen Dietz, business storytelling author, coach, facilitator (USA)

"Mary Alice draws on a lifetime of work with stories and offers a year's worth of nourishments for your soul. This inspiring yet down-to-earth book reflects her global connections, her strong heart, and her generous spirit. Enjoy it today and the next day…"

David Drake, PhD, author of *Narrative Coaching: The Definitive Guide to Bringing New Stories to Life* (USA)

"*365 ALIVE!* is a beautiful invitation into our human capacity to make meaning and to make story and as we take up the pen in the writing of our lives, human aliveness will visit us with all its magic and wonder."

Chené Swart, author of *Re-authoring the World: The Narrative Lens and Practices for Organisations, Communities and Individuals* (South Africa)

"It's my experience that just one conversation with Mary Alice can be transformative — and through the reflections and actions she offers in *365 ALIVE!* you gift yourself an entire year of benefiting from her wisdom and guidance!"

Thaler Pekar, internationally recognized pioneer in communication and narrative (USA)

"Anyone who has ever worked with Mary Alice knows the depth and wisdom with which she radiates her magic. With *365 ALIVE!* she now lets us share in this magic. 'Story' as we can learn here is more than just telling stories. Story can be a companion, inspirer, door opener, gamechanger and leader. It's good to have that in your luggage — as host, facilitator and leader in times like these."

Holger Scholz, Natural Facilitator, Kommunikationslotsen (Germany)

"Mary Alice brilliantly weaves together her ability to play with story, her mastery of asking questions and her skill in crafting unique invitations to invite you into your own stories at multiple layers to bring you more and more into yourself. So get this book. Read it and be curious about your story and yourself."

Quanita Roberson, Organizational Shaman (USA)

"This book is certainly a call to the special world. An irresistible invitation to go on your own hero's journey in which you will be given new ears and eyes for the multitude of stories, the joy of telling, the power of listening and the insight that narration can change reality."

Hanna Lundblad, scriptwriter and creator of *The Seaside Hotel* (Denmark)

"I had no idea this book was missing for me, until I started to read it. Now I will have it close to my heart to develop my personal life story. I will use the questions in the book to develop my peers and loved ones. And, I will use it in my profession as a facilitator to change perspectives, move forwards and change the world."

Jonas Roth Sjöblom, PhD, Space Creator and Master Facilitator (Sweden)

"Mary Alice has pilgrimed the field of stories for decades now. She guides you into story — yours, ours and what might be. Pay closest attention to Part 3. Listening, witnessing, and staying present are the capacities we lack most in the so-called developed world. In this time of collapse and regeneration, we will find our way forward best by listening with every fiber of our being. Take your time with *365 ALIVE!* Let it soak into you and become a new friend."

Bob Stilger, author of *AfterNow: When We Cannot See the Future, Where Do We Begin?* (USA)

"This book is an opportunity to explore beyond the obvious. It's a story about stories and a self-guided workshop inside our own stories. Over the course of fifty-two weeks, Mary Alice Arthur inspires with insights, learnings, and exercises to help us grow from within to become better versions of ourselves, and showing that storytelling goes beyond the story. *365 ALIVE!* is not only about the art and craft of storytelling but about a new perspective on life."

Dr. Myriam Hadnes, podcaster and founder, Workshops Work (The Netherlands)

"Mary Alice Arthur's new book is a tour de force — more than just a manual, this is how story ways can transform your life, one day at a time. She teaches from her own experience, so in Mary Alice we have a reliable guide leading us into a year that will make a difference."

Paul Costello, founder of Storywise.com, Executive Director, AmeriCorps Project CHANGE (USA)

"We live by the stories we tell ourselves — and we create the world by the stories we share with others. *365 ALIVE!* takes us on a journey into the richness and depths of working with story — your own, the communities you are part of and beyond. The labor, love and practical wisdom that went into this book make it an outstanding contribution to the field. A go-to guide to develop and hone your skills and tools in working with stories, develop your practice and grow your impact."

Jacques Chlopczyk, Beyond Storytelling Network (Germany)

"Mary Alice Arthur stands out as a most dedicated human being and as a rare story artist in service of us all living more consciously and humanely together. She gracefully weaves the threads of the ancient and ever-fresh patterns of our stories into something more and useful in the day-to-day of our lives. If you are seeking to understand yourself and to understand the other through the beauty, strength and inspiration of practising story and not just hear them, but truly open up and listen to what they offer — here is a unique exploration for you."

Toke Paludan Møller, co-founder of Art of Hosting, The Flow Game, and the Practising for Peace Dojo (Denmark)

"This book goes down like homemade lemonade during a hot summer afternoon. You quickly witness Mary Alice's stunning ability to craft powerful questions that inspire you to a wholehearted reflection and give rise to skillful action. A must-read book for anyone who wants to delve into the transformational power of storytelling and enrich the path of their lives with a deep sense of purpose. After taking this journey, as Mary Alice says, 'Things will never be the same again.'"

Yannis Angelis, contributor to *Transforming Organizations: Narrative and Story-Based Approaches* (Germany)

"This book is a doorway to not only experience how story can help one realize and actualize our relationship with the world, but also the deep connection to who we are. Reading this visual, personal, and evocative guide allows us to connect with how story creates meaning. It is a personal, powerful, and even painful journey when we experience the fifty-two skillfully designed instructional landscapes that Arthur presents to us. She is there to remind us this is a journey worth taking."

Kevin D. Cordi, Ph.D., Storytelling Chair, National Council Teachers of English (USA)

"*365 ALIVE!* is a conversation between Mary Alice Arthur and her readers inviting us to probe into, question and become wiser about our own stories and those around us, so that we can become more aware and free to choose the life we want to live and the world we wish to create. She has paved the way for us through her deep work and rich experience with storytelling, but what I love about *365 ALIVE!* is we have to dive in ourselves and do the work to change our stories — and when we do, the rewards are amazing."

Anne Christine Hagedorn, facilitator and author of *Your Inner Climate* (Denmark)

"No social transformation exists without individual change and vice versa. The *365 ALIVE!* journey starts by focusing on the reader and on her or his story. With this foundation established, the invitation is to look outwards, to how stories work in the world and activate their positive power to foster compassion, respect for differences, creativity, solidarity, cooperation, and resilience. The stories we are telling to explain the global crisis are diverse and contradictory. We are in a collective crossroad and choices must be made without any certainty. During this dangerous navigation towards uncharted shores, we can use the power of stories to deal with paradox and connect with others in love, extracting kindness and beauty out of the apparent chaos."

Madza Ednir, activist, communicator and educator for Global Citizenship (Brazil)

"A resonance rings out in Mary Alice Arthur's gentle understanding that the Storyteller's role has never been to make the meaning 'simple,' but to find comfort in the complexity of All. There has always been a need for mapping, sense-making, witnessing, being both heard, listened to and present; but, when stories are seen in relation and service to our social nature and need for community, she serves up an invitation and welcoming to share."

Dovie Thomasen, professional storyteller (USA)

"Mary Alice Arthur has long been a voice of empathy-powered wisdom in the world. At last, with *365 ALIVE!*, her voice is accessible to everyone … and for a full fifty-two weeks of compassionate self discovery. This is an extravagant gift, and I hope everyone will receive it."

David Hutchens, author, *Circle of the 9 Muses* and *Story Sprint* (USA)

"There are so many elements and levels to this book that it surprised me. But of course, stories create our lives and make sense of our lives. As Mary Alice writes: 'Change your story — change the world.' As a sustainability advisor I have learnt the power of stories, the power of imagination. If you want to create a sustainable world you must first imagine it, create the story about and of it. Then you can realise it. *365 ALIVE!* is a great practical guide to work with stories from the outside in and inside out, where you become wiser as you immerse yourself in the story universe. Our world needs a new story, a new dream. *365 ALIVE!* can help facilitate it."

Karen Blincoe, Ph.D., Advisor Sustainability, FRSA, DD (Denmark)

"For years I have been a student and practitioner of storytelling, going back to my business school days. I am so thrilled to see this culmination of Mary Alice's years of work in the storytelling space in *365 ALIVE!* Part 1 of the book explains the purpose, logic, cadence and potential of this book. Part 2 focuses on giving good insights for developing one's own personal story. Part 3 examines how one's story can be used in our work as professionals, managers and leaders. Part 4 carries us into how we use our story to create the future world that we most want to fruition. If you're a story practitioner or a student this book will significantly sharpen your saw."

Craig DeLarge, MBA, CPC, Strategist at The Digital Mental Health Project (USA)

"*365 ALIVE!* offers us an invitation. We can, if we choose, become more aware and more awake. We can move from being a reactor to a creator. We can become the author of our own life story. It provides a clear weekly framework to work on ways to live a deeply conscious life, aware of our own stories and the stories of others. Resting on a solid theoretical base using the collective wisdom of many historical and cultural traditions, this book is a call to action. The author has done so much of the hard work for us. So, even though it is a book of challenges, we, like heroes in the old tales, are offered many helping hands, gifts and surprising suggestions along the way. Following the path set out in this book would be a rewarding way to spend a year but the process itself is an enriching work with enough actions to last a lifetime."

Gill Di Stefano, Professional Storyteller (Australia)

I haven't done all the practices Mary Alice proposes, but those I have done have helped me understand the deeper meaning of a story I have been telling myself since I was nine and at the same time to tell it in a new way, so that it points towards a much warmer and lighter place than I have ever seen before. I am not anymore about bringing light to dark and cold places, but about kindling a campfire whose warmth and light invites those who live in cold and dark places to sit with us. Sitting by the campfire, I hear Mary Alice telling her stories…

Eugenio Moliní, your partner in change (Sweden)

"This book is written to us as a love letter to stories and storytellers. It's an exquisite invitation to be archaeologists of story — for ourselves to deepen our own lives, and for these times, to imagine the stories we can live into collectively. With joy and mastery, depth and originality, Mary Alice Arthur illuminates the art of excavating and participating in the StoryField. She reminds us that we are the stories we tell. We have the power to create memories, live in our present, and become our futures. Our lives, quite literally, depend on it."

Vanessa Reid, co-founder, The Living Wholeness Institute (Canada)

Alive! 365

Alive! 365

Find your voice. Claim your story.
Live your brilliant life.

MARY ALICE ARTHUR

Foreword by Juanita Brown

365 ALIVE! Find your voice. Claim your story. Live your brilliant life.

Copyright © Mary Alice Arthur 2020
Foreword copyright © Juanita Brown 2020
All rights reserved.

Published by Firelight, PO Box 21510, Columbus, Ohio 43221, USA

All rights reserved. No part of this publication may be reproduced, stored in a retrieval system, communicated or transmitted in any form or by any means, electronic, mechanical, photocopying, recoding, scanning, or otherwise, except as permitted under Section 107 or 108 of the 1976 United States Copyright Act, without either the prior written permission, or authorization through payment of the appropriate per-copy fee. All inquiries should be made to the author.

Library of Congress Control Number: 2020923632

First printing, December 2020
ISBN 978-1-7359586-7-5 (paperback); ISBN 978-1-7359586-0-6 (cloth);
ISBN 978-1-7359586-1-3 (ePub)

Cover design: Sumit Shringi
Cover image: Based on an image by Tomáš Malík (@malcoo on Unsplash)
Text design: Avril Orloff

DISCLAIMER

This book provides general information, discussion and practical suggestions about storytelling and related subjects. The words and other content provided in this book, and in any linked materials, are not intended and should not be construed as psychological advice. If the reader or any other person has a psychological or medical concern, s/he should consult with an appropriately-licensed therapist, physician or other healthcare worker. Please use your own good judgement in taking any actions that may relate to this material. Neither the author nor the publisher shall be liable or responsible for any loss or damage allegedly arising from any information or suggestions in this book.

DEDICATION

To those of you who are journeyers, this is an invitation. Can you see that flickering fire over there? You'll find us waiting for you. We are the storytellers, the saga singers, the bards, the griots, the tellers of tales. We are your ancestors, your lineage holders, your teachers, your family. We are heroes and tricksters, old wise ones and bumbling fools. We are saints and sinners, royalty and rabble. We are magicians and alchemists. We are shapeshifters. We haunt the corridors of time, and conjure it to stand still, speed up, behave in mysterious ways. We are your birthright, your treasure, the legacy of humanity. And we are those who come after, those who long for the learning and nourishment only story can bring. We are those who call you to remember. It's time to uncover who you are, let go of what's no longer needed and dream what might be. And together, choose how we will bring life to our stories and our stories to life.

If you ask me what a story really is, here's what I'd say:

A story is heard and a story is told
a story is subtle, a story is bold,
a story is mood and a story is pace
and sometimes a story, well, it's full of grace.

A story is you and a story is me
a story is truth and a story is free.
A story is history, mystery, song,
and you're all invited so come sing along!

Some stories are large and some they are small,
just like some people are short, some are tall.
Some stories are old friends, and some they are new
just take them all in, it's the best thing to do.

Some stories bring laughter, and some they bring tears
to hear when you're strong or to quiet your fears
to give you some courage when you're at a low
and sometimes a story will help you to grow.

It'll take you new places and bring you right home,
'cause stories go with you wherever you roam.
And stories are needed to keep the world new,
'cause Imagination's the nation that we belong to.

A story is like a whole kingdom of flowers —
some sweet and precious, and some with great powers.
And just like a human gets joy from a flower,
a story will give you the gift of its power.

So gather 'round people and take what you need —
go plant a garden, I'll give you a seed.

CONTENTS

FOREWORD — i

INTRODUCTION: WELCOME TO *365 ALIVE!* — 1

PART ONE: GETTING STARTED WITH STORY — 13

1. Taking curiosity as your starting point — 15
2. Stories are the currency of humanity — 19
3. Make a story health check — 25
4. What stories have you been steeping in? — 29

PART TWO: MAPPING YOUR PERSONAL STORYFIELD — 33

5. How can stories help you take an eagle-eye view? — 35
6. What stories are shaping your stance in the world? — 41
7. What stories are you living up to? — 45
8. How are your stories shaping your memories? — 49
9. What stories do you want to relive? — 53
10. How can stories help you understand life? — 57
11. Where are your beginnings, middles and endings right now? — 61
12. Which of your stories needs to breathe? — 65
13. How is "not-knowing" offering you a new view of your story? — 69
14. What movement could make all the difference to your story? — 73
15. What will you decide to make out of what happened to you? — 77
16. Is your life telling the story you want to tell? — 81
17. What pain needs its story told? — 85
18. What are the truthful stories that need to be shared now? — 89

19	What story will unleash what is waiting inside you?	93
20	Who do you want to be and how can your story help you get there?	97
21	What story can help you experience what you dream of?	101
22	Which of your stories is waiting to be told?	105
23	What is your story of everyday courage?	109
24	What can you learn through taking a mythic view of your life?	113
25	What stuck story needs to change?	117
26	What question could change your life?	121
27	How can slowing down help you see more?	127
28	What seeds do you want to water now?	131

PART THREE: STORY AT WORK IN THE WORLD — 135

29	Stories help us make meaning	139
30	Stories make sense	143
31	Stories give us connection	147
32	Stories are a frame for imaginative possibility	151
33	Stories help us honor and integrate our woundings	155
34	Stories help us take back our power	161
35	Stories help us reclaim ourselves	165
36	Stories help us remember who we are	169
37	Stories help us share the incredible	175
38	Stories awaken possibilities	179
39	Stories are healing	183
40	Stories help us to meet	187
41	Stories are way showers	193
42	Stories help us care for and hold each other	197
43	Stories are our collective responsibility	201

PART FOUR: YOUR FUTURE STORY — 207

| 44 | What stories help to resource you? | 209 |
| 45 | Which stories remind you to find and follow your bliss? | 213 |

46	How can story help you find and embrace your superpower?	217
47	What story will keep you going no matter what?	221
48	How can stories impact your choices for the better?	225
49	What stories can bring your dream to life?	229
50	How can your story empower you to act?	233
51	What story can help you transform?	237
52	What is your story in the making?	241

REMEMBER — YOUR STORY MATTERS! **245**

EPILOGUE **247**

FOOTNOTES **253**

ILLUSTRATIONS **258**

GRATITUDE **261**

INDEX **262**

AUTHOR **267**

FOREWORD

To My Son: Born in a Time of Coronavirus and Climate Change

So this will be your first life lesson, little River: We are human and unlike all the other animals, we are made of stories. Our big brain's ability to imagine different realities and communicate new ideas to our children, neighbors and millions of strangers is what makes us the most powerful force in the known universe. Stories! EVERYTHING in our man-made world — flags and borders, money and markets, laws and religions — all of it came from the stories we tell ourselves.

Bill Weir, CNN Chief Climate Correspondent

When Mary Alice and I met more than a decade ago, I was struck by her passion around the power of individual and collective story sharing as well as her unique approach to "story harvesting." I was impressed by her use of the framework of "story activism" — activating empowering stories that can lead us to more flourishing futures, both in our own lives as well as in the larger world.

Coming from a family legacy of activism, the name itself evoked memories of key stories that have shaped my own life journey. Mary Alice caused me to think, for the first time, about stories that had been key to discovering my own identity as a leadership strategist devoted to the co-evolution of life-affirming futures in organizations and communities.

I recalled the stories I witnessed during my years working with Cesar Chavez and the farmworkers movement in California. Over bean suppers in ramshackle homes with cracked linoleum floors, workers shared the stories of their lives and their determination to somehow create a better future for their children and grandchildren.

Folks from one house meeting would help organize others, expanding the sharing and weaving of stories from one home to another. The Farmworkers Theater, *El Teatro Campesino*, listened deeply. In their performances at large farmworker gatherings, they created a new image of possibility for farmworkers to tell their grandchildren — of the days when the old story of poverty and discrimination ended and a new story was being born.

Using only masks, small placards, sunglasses, bandanas and their capacity for improvisational humor, El Teatro reflected back, amplified and enriched — like a mirror with microphones — the life of farmworkers and the absurdity of the predicament that farmworkers, or anyone for that matter, should even have to struggle for basic things like the right to toilets in the fields.

The people watched. The people listened, and the people responded. They engaged actively in beginning to transform a story of despair to a story of desire for constructive change. Farmworkers and hundreds of thousands of their allies in cities across the nation responded with courage and collective action. A new story was born as those laboring in the fields achieved the very first worker agreements with growers in the history of American agriculture — a story that continues to give some hope of progress to farmworkers across the nation.

Thirty years later, in 1995, the World Café approach to large-scale collaborative dialogue was born by accident in our living room with twenty-four global thought leaders. As we reflected on what we'd experienced that fateful day, Finn Voldtofte, our Danish friend and colleague who first named the World Café, shared his prescient observation that what we'd experienced as a surprise that rainy morning was "a pattern of engagement born into the world for world service."

It was not until a decade later that a group of corporate executives in that same living room asked me what I thought had enabled the amazing spread of the World Café to six continents. It suddenly dawned on me that the World Café pattern of moving from one table to another, cross-pollinating ideas and sharing individual stories from which new collective possibilities emerged, was the *same* pattern I'd observed in the spreading of the farmworker house meetings — the connection of individual stories birthing new collective possibilities, creating a sense that each person had a voice and choice in determining the stories that would shape their lives.

We once again witnessed the power of story as Mary Alice and I shared experiences at the Staging Change programs I was co-facilitating in collaboration with the International Storytelling Center (www.storytellingcenter.net) in Jonesborough, Tennessee. The Storytelling Center has helped to shape the global revival of storytelling both as an art form and as an active platform for their mission of "building a better world through stories."

Each of these formative stories in my own life has enabled me to experience the power of narrative as the connective tissue linking our personal stories with the stories of our times. They have reinforced Mary Alice's core message in her book, ***365 ALIVE!*** — the core message that each of us has the power to discover whether the stories we live by today make us prisoners of our past or pioneers of our future.

This uniquely organized and designed book makes a special contribution, not only to our individual and collective evolution, but also to the field of storytelling and story sharing itself. The field has gained growing acceptance as we've learned how our brains process information, create coherent narratives, and make meaning of our lives through the stories we tell ourselves and those that shape our views of the world around us.

The power of story as a core process for shaping our futures shines through each page as Mary Alice takes us on a journey of discovery, integrating self and society. Like peeling back the layers of an onion, Mary Alice takes us deeper — connecting intimacy and scale. We become aware of the stories that have shaped our own lives as well as the challenges and opportunities of the stories we live by — recognizing that we can take back the power of our stories to shape futures worthy of our best effort.

Mary Alice invites us to engage with compassion for ourselves and others in a year-long personal learning journey of disciplined practices that allow us to discover the "source stories" and "turning-point stories" that have shaped our personal perceptions of ourselves and the world around us.

Each of its fifty-two sections includes powerful and probing questions that Mary Alice asks us to ponder. They provide the opportunity not only to become aware of the stories we tell ourselves, but open the doorway for us to take back the power of our stories in order to shape more life-affirming futures — for ourselves and for our wounded world.

I had a dear friend in Mexico whom I asked why the word for question in Spanish was feminine, *pregunta*, and he answered, "because questions are always pregnant with possibilities!"

Throughout this book Mary Alice's provocative questions struck me to my core. She enabled me to see how pregnant with possibilities the use of story can be, particularly now, as we live in this transformative time of "not knowing." The COVID-19 crisis has provided the challenge as well as the opportunity to reassess the stories of who we have been and the stories of who we now want to become. The story of the death of George Floyd, a story heard round the world, is a story that has evoked both strong emotions as well as the possibility of systemic change. The story of the impact of climate change on our communities is awakening a generation of young people to raise their voices and their hearts, asking us all to live into a more generative story than the one preordained by our current unsustainable trajectory.

These stories of our lives are raising more questions than answers — yet we are early in the process of living into them as seeds for change. As the poet Rainer Maria Rilke shared with a young poet who had asked him for advice, "try to love the questions themselves" and "live into" the answers as life-affirming paths forward become more visible.

I feel blessed and honored to be Mary Alice's friend and colleague as we each embody the use of story in our mutual hosting of participatory practices.

Storytelling, story sharing, and story harvesting have been and will be at the heart of these collaborative ways of evoking collective intelligence and wise action around the complex challenges we face as a human community in these troubled times.

Juanita Brown, PhD
Co-founder of World Café
Co-author with David Isaacs and the World Café Community, *The World Café: Shaping our Futures Through Conversations that Matter*
Co-author, *Story Bridge: From Alienation to Community Action*

> We live in a story
> ・・・
> and that means we can **CHANGE** it.
>
> — Mary Alice Arthur, *Story Activist*

Welcome to *365 ALIVE!*

Thank you for joining me on the story journey!

I've loved stories all my life. I didn't hear that many at home, but I was an avid reader who adored the school library. There were times I walked to school reading two books at once. Thank goodness I lived in a flat place! Eventually this passion took me to the first storytelling festival in New Zealand and there I discovered the magic of oral storytelling. I saw a very gifted storyteller mesmerize the group and take us all on a very emotional journey. "What just happened?" I asked myself. And a split second later: "I wonder if I can do that?"

Back in the library again, I stuffed myself full of folktales, fairytales, myths and legends and became a storyteller. I soon realized hearing my own voice was not enough; I wanted to hear others' stories too. That took me into working with groups and using story as part of my process. Hosting groups has taken me all over the world. Through my travels, I've heard enough stories to know that we humans are story creatures. Sharing stories is how we connect to each other — and ourselves.

Some time ago, I began putting quotes I'd collected about story and life together with images. Playing with the text and the graphics was fun! It reawakened the "cut and paste" passion of my childhood, when I loved working with paper, scissors and glue. I began to imagine 365 of these creations — enough for a year's worth of daily inspiration. Working on them during a particularly challenging time in my life saved me from sinking. I found myself wanting to build on the doorways they make and this book is one of the results of my work.

Although I made more than 365 quotes, in the end I chose fifty-two of them to form the core of this year-long journey into story. I decided that a weekly focus would allow readers to discover how stories can become companions and allies, a light to all the days of the year.

365 ALIVE! is about coming truly alive in your life

As a storyteller and story practitioner, I've realized that what makes the difference to success or failure is determined by the stories we tell ourselves and each other. Our stories help us make sense and meaning of the world and through this lens we are either hindered or empowered to take action. Our stories are key to whether we believe we have agency[1] in this world or not. They make the difference to whether we feel powerless or powerful and whether we can step up to take action and make an impact.

Try on the idea that you live inside a story

Your story came partially from your culture and context and somewhat from your family and a lot from how you decided to interpret the events that happened to you. Eventually a story can become either a doorway to something new or a prison of the past. But the key to the door is choosing to face the story, challenge the meaning and change.

The business of stories is about waking up and making conscious choices to shape the stories that shape you. That is also the business of *365 ALIVE!* This journey is about waking up and taking back the power of your story.

When you wake up to the stories at work in your life you suddenly step into the position of power. You can choose how you make meaning of your past and how you step forward into the future. You can choose how your story unfolds and how you make sense of the world. Story stops being what defines you and becomes your ally — *you become a* **Story Activist** *in your own life.*

What is a Story Activist?

I define a Story Activist as someone who works with the stories of people, places and things to discover and activate their greatest potential. You can be

a Story Activist for yourself, too. In plain speak, that means **activating** the stories that lead you to a more flourishing future.

Which stories help you thrive? Where are your stories keeping you stuck? What story could liberate you? Where can story help you to move first to new ground, and from there to higher ground? What stories can help you work with others to create your most flourishing future together?

These are the questions a Story Activist asks. I hope they will become your questions, too.

It is time to wake up to the way stories work. It is time to become vigilant.

A story colleague of mine[2] talks about the space between your ears as being the most important real estate on the planet. Every day, and from every direction, you are bombarded with stories seeking to come and live in your head. Some of them are hiding in conversations with friends and colleagues, some are shared in families or common interest groups, some come through advertising, media and the internet, some through religion, politics or opinions. *They are everywhere!*

Our stories can hold us down or they can lift us up. We can choose.

— MARY ALICE ARTHUR

So begin by learning how stories work. How are they impacting you? Which of them support you to be the person you want to be and live your most fulfilled life?

Then become vigilant. We have the opportunity to choose which stories we want to react to, live with and live in. Pay attention today to the stories you are hearing. How many of them are true? How many are generative? What do they tell you about the meaning you and others are making out of what you are experiencing? This is a time to be discerning and aware in your choices.

Being on the *365 ALIVE!* journey

365 ALIVE! is a fifty-two-week exploration of how story works around you and within you. It will take you on a journey to your depths and your edges. It will be confirming, in places challenging, sometimes painful and often rewarding.

Sometimes it will feel like digging in the basement and sometimes it will be like reaching into the heights. Both are important and each is needed as a balance to the other. You can't fly high without foundations to give you solid ground to take off from. This work is created to hold up a mirror to the stories you are carrying and those at work around you.

It may feel like peeling an onion, as we return to revisit some themes more deeply. This is a good thing. Stories need time to unfold and you need time to learn to trust them, and yourself, more fully.

Each week you'll be presented with the stimulus of an image and a quote, as well as suggestions on how to work with what the quote prompts in you. There are three parts to this. First you'll have something to read in the **THINK ABOUT** section. The text offers some thoughts on the week's stimulus.

Next you'll see **TAKE ACTION**. Here are some tasks for you to take on. Sometimes you'll be asked to work directly with your story, some of the tasks aim to build your awareness and some challenge you to take action or build a new habit. Finally there is the **HAVE A LOOK** section where I offer links to videos, books or movies which reinforce the theme or give you a new perspective.

There are four parts to this year of activity

We start in **Part One** by listening in to stories around us. What can we learn about the StoryField[3] in which we live and work? What happens when we are more aware of what is happening around us, rather than just letting it flow over or through us? *This is our "getting started" time and lasts for four weeks.*

In **Part Two** we take a longer time delving into our own stories and what they mean. We put the focus on where we want to take them and where we want them to take us. This is the longest part of our journey — almost half our time together! *We spend twenty-four weeks working with your personal stories.*

In **Part Three** we turn the lens on the way stories are working in the world and how stories work between people. Both of these perspectives are needed if you want to activate and foster new insight or change with others. *We focus on a different aspect of what stories can do each week for a total of fifteen weeks.*

Part Four takes us into the future story. Where does your story go from here? What do you intend to transform in your stories and in your life? *These final nine weeks bring us to the conclusion of our fifty-two weeks of story.*

How to use this book

365 ALIVE! begins with an invitation to take on the practice of StoryWork for fifty-two weeks. Something important happens when you make a commitment with yourself — one might say a contract — for a certain amount of time. When you make a commitment, something deeper and more authentic can show up. Making a commitment requires courage, the courage of being willing to go through the fire for yourself. Telling yourself you are there for you no matter what means you can really show up. You are creating the inner space for deep practice. Be aware that very few people do this. AND it makes all the difference!

Each week builds on the last and is intended to be worked in order, but this is not a hard and fast rule. Use your intuition. If you believe you need to start somewhere else, if you like dipping in and seeing what shows up, do that.

Work in the way that most suits you.

If you want to build a habit with this work you can keep, then choose a specific time. Maybe you want to do your story work on Sunday mornings. Maybe you are a Tuesday evening kind of person. Regular timing makes it easier to stay with a practice.

Each week invites you to keep the focus it offers for the entire week. When you open yourself to stay focused on something, more appears for you to work with. You might want to write the question or statement for the week on a sticky note and put it on your bathroom mirror or on your fridge. You might

> We make our lives bigger or smaller, more expansive or more limited, according to the interpretation of life that is our *Story.*
> CHRISTINA BALDWIN, "STORYCATCHER"

want to set your screensaver with the statement or write a prompt in your calendar. The more curiosity you apply, the more you will receive in return.

Be both fierce and gentle with yourself

My advice is to make a commitment to yourself to keep going. This is not easy work. Therefore be fierce. Make a commitment to your practice time and stick with it. Keep going even when it feels hard. And, be **gentle**. Story work is tender work. It can be challenging to see things about yourself you don't like or to know that you are not where you want to be … yet. And it can be confronting to be faced with your own potential — even if that's what you think you want. If you need to take a break, do that; just come back when you can and keep going.

Some people find it easier to stay committed if they have a buddy or an accountability partner working with them. Is there someone else you'd like to share this work and experience with? It will be even richer!

This is not intended to be a therapy book, even though working with story is therapeutic. It is wise to have a close friend or partner, or a circle of people who can help to hold you during the time you do this work. When you need help or an outside perspective, ask for it. The Western cultural story teaches us that we need to be strong and self-sufficient. This is a story that needs changing! When we ask for help, we give others the opportunity to gift to us so we can be a gift in return. Ask for what you need!

And remember: Stories need time to grow in you and time to be released as well. Resistance is a sure sign there's something here to be learned. Be fierce about your practice and gentle with yourself.

Ready to get started?

You have what you need inside you. Your own life is a source of rich content for you to work with. It is the foundation for everything you are and

How can our Stories help us discover our potentials and possibilities together? Which stories do we need to look at in a new way? Which no longer serve? How can we -- as individuals, groups and collectives -- take back the power of our Stories and use them for good?

MARY ALICE ARTHUR

will be in this world, because your stories are like a lens, influencing how you see life, and therefore, what action you will take. You don't need to love — or even like — some of your stories. All you need to do is accept them and be open to what they might offer you in your journey.

The first step is to become aware you are a multiplicity of stories.

Remember, you are not a single story, *you are an intersection of stories.* That means you can look at your life and your stories from different angles and there will always be something new to see. For example:

- *What are the stories of your family background? Your ethnicity or place?*

- *What did you learn about how families work and what constituted success? What did you learn about gender roles or how someone should approach life?*
- *Who supported you? Who challenged you?*
- *Who or what sparked joy or anger or confidence, or any other response from you and why?*

Begin writing down your stories. You'll want to find a journal or a notebook to dedicate to this work. You might want to write down a list of questions to ask yourself or create a list of headings like *Work, Family, Love, Success, Relationships, Travel,* and so on. Just start writing anywhere.

Keep on writing them as they pop up in your head or heart. Use the upcoming quotes as stimuli. Listen to other people's stories and see what they trigger in you. Explore yourself with the grace and curiosity you would a new and much-valued friend or loved one. Be gentle with yourself, and nevertheless, persistent. One practice you might want to take on is writing a story a day. Doing this is like creating a story muscle. With practice, it becomes ever easier.

This is not about perfection. It's not about writing a "good" story. It is about finding out about the stories you are living in. Only then can you make a choice.

In the mirror. *Yep, you heard me!* Take a look at the person whose story is the most important one in the world to you. You are worth this time investment and whatever it will uncover. Take a least a full minute to look into your own eyes and tell yourself you are worth this exploration and you're looking forward to getting to know yourself better. Assure yourself you are there for you, you are committed to honoring your stories. *How does that feel?*

Thank you for beginning!

Stories *have been at work* within you since before you were born. You are the intersection of all the stories others hold about you and you hold about yourself. All the stories of family, culture, place, belief and experience -- *a veritable StoryField of meaning and potentiality.*

What will you do with what you've been given?

MARY ALICE ARTHUR

PART ONE

Getting Started with Story

Think for a moment about the stories of your life. There have been so many! What is your founding story? Which stories have shaped you into the person you are today? What are you grateful for, what are you still challenged by and what have you learned as a result?

It's time to put the focus on how stories are a part of being human. Your own life is a treasure trove of story. From before the time you were born, stories swirled around you and began to shape who you would become. Even before you had language you created meaning out of your experiences. Every day, new stories arise and you decide how they fit into your view of yourself and the world.

Everyone is given the same amount of time in a day, but what they make with it depends on the stories they hold about it. *What will you do with what you have been given?*

Become awake to how stories are at work. Even as you are shaping your stories, your stories are shaping you. It sounds like a good partnership — but is it? The first step is to begin the exploration of how stories work and how they influence you. A growing awareness puts you in the driver's seat, more able to take charge and steer your life.

In Part 1 we will delve into story at work in the world. We begin our journey by evoking curiosity, one of the greatest tools of the storyteller. We take a look at story as the currency of humanity and use stories to do a health check of the systems around us. And finally we take a first look at the stories you've been living in. These first four weeks are dedicated to waking up our appreciation and awareness of stories.

Welcome to the journey. Let's take our first steps down the road!

WEEK 1
Taking curiosity as your starting point

Think about...

Curiosity is a basic human quality and an essential tool for a storyteller.

Curiosity is an opening door, a beckoning pathway, the niggle that makes you turn in a new direction. Why have you begun this journey with yourself? What is it about stories — and your own story in particular — that makes you curious? What do you hope to find as a result?

Curiosity is an important starting point because when you are curious about something, you want to explore it. Explorers start with a premise, but they know they don't yet know the answer. They do what they can to prepare themselves, getting the right equipment together, looking for a skilled team, spreading out the map. They chart a course, but they also know that what they discover along the way will impact both the direction and the depth of the journey. They are prepared to be surprised and keen to make discoveries. **They know the map is not the territory.** They want to find something new, but are also aware they may need to leave something old behind. That means curiosity is one of the prime practices for both explorers and storytellers.

Well-traveled people know that it makes sense only to carry with you what is useful or important. The rest is just baggage. As you explore, you will realize that some of your old stories are not useful or important to you, and you may choose to leave them by the side of the road.

This is a moment on the archetypal crossroads, a moment where the (s)hero makes a choice to go on a journey. The crossroads is a place in imagination where many stories begin. It's helpful to know what your starting point is.

 Take action...

Get prepared. If you haven't before now, find a story journal or notebook and something to write with. Your journal might also be online. Taking regular stock of what's going on inside you is a great way to help yourself digest and integrate what you're learning.

Decide who your team will be on this journey. Is there a partner or friend you want to check in with on a regular basis to share how it's going? Or are you someone who has an imaginal boardroom where you meet with mentors or helpers?

Perhaps you are working with a coach or a therapist. Including them on your team makes good sense for moving forward well. Having a support team is helpful when the going gets tough or you uncover something surprising.

Finally, decide when you will dedicate time to this work, make a commitment to yourself and your team and get going.

Think back to a time when you were young and curious. Every child is endlessly curious; that's probably the reason they ask "Why?" so often! Think back to a moment in your younger days when you felt you were bursting with curiosity and energy. If you can't find that time in memory, imagine yourself in this state. Got the picture in your head? Really sense the energy of your younger self. Put out your left hand, palm up, and imagine your younger self standing there.

Now imagine yourself at the end of this year-long journey, one year older, but wiser than you are now. That wiser one is radiating with energy and vitality, and has plenty to share. Put out your right hand, palm up, and imagine your wise elder standing there.

> Curiosity is one of the prime practices for a storyteller. This is a moment on the archetypal crossroads, where a new story can begin.

Get some support for the journey. Have a conversation with your younger and older selves. Ask them:

- What do you know about life that I need to remember?
- What wisdom can you share about the journey I'm about to go on?
- What gift(s) do you have for me that will support me in my journey?
- What is your advice to me on this journey?

Before turning to your journal to make some notes, thank your other selves for their contribution. Bring your palms together to combine the energy of curious younger self and wiser older self for the journey ahead.

What journey story can give you courage to make your own journey? Explore and find one. You might love the ancient Greek heroes like Jason and the Argonauts, or Ulysses. Maybe you're a fan of the Arctic or Antarctic explorers. Perhaps you favor the scientific explorations of a Madame Curie or Nikola Tesla, or those who are exploring the reaches of outer space or inner psychology. Maybe you thrill to the worldwide voyages of the Chinese or the Vikings, or those who are creating fusions of the arts. Maybe you honor the stories of those who left their homelands or were taken away to make new lives somewhere else. Whose journey story inspires you?

Find one this week and let it sit with you. Make some journal notes about why this particular story inspires you and what you are learning from it as you turn to it during the week.

WEEK 2
Stories are the currency of humanity

 **Think about...**

Someone once said that the most common form of travel on the planet is by opening a book.

Stories travel across borders of all kinds. They are the currency we trade with each other as humans. While you might not meet others around the fire or the well today, you make space to trade stories over coffee, around the computer, over the internet, through your phone, while shopping, when learning — any time you interact with another human you share stories with each other …

We are literally awash with stories. They surround us from the moment we open our eyes in the morning until we go to bed at night, and then they pursue us into our dreams.

Think about it. You sit on your front step or on your balcony having coffee and you look into the community story that surrounds you. Is this a place that is thriving or one that is challenged? Are there opportunities for people like you in the place where you live? Is it a safe place or a dangerous one? All of this is impacted by the stories people hold about the place — *and each other.*

Then you get ready for the day. Most likely the phone you are holding has a story attached to it. So do the clothes you put on or the shoes you choose. How you get to work is a story. Do you run for the bus or train or ride a bike? Do you walk? Is your work in the next room or on your lap in the form of a computer? Are you walking into a corporate story? Are you taking care of your kids and therefore inside the story of parenting? Or do you work for yourself, attempting to thrive at the crossroads of how you see yourself and how others see you? Or maybe you don't have a job and you're wondering what to do now. There's a story in itself.

In every newscast, in every magazine, in every internet posting, stories are alive and we are creating them together. How aware can you become of their influence on your life? How awake can you become to the stories you are living in?

If the most important real estate on the planet is the space between your ears, stories will always try to come and live there. That makes good food for thought — which stories will you let live rent-free in your head?

It has been said that there is no innocent story. Every story has an intention, even if it is told with innocence. Stories ask for something: "See me!", "Feel with me!", "Help me understand what I've experienced!" **So, what is the currency you are exchanging? What is the intention behind the stories *you* share?**

For the coming week, don't take any story for granted. Pay close attention to the stories around you. What do you notice? What kind of currency is being shared? If an old friend phones you, what character are you playing in the story? If you listen to a story at work, why is the story being told?

Pay attention to people. Start by remembering that everyone lives inside the lens of their own stories. We each see the world through the stories we use to create meaning. Many people can experience the same event and see it totally differently. When ten people experience something, you can be guaranteed there will be at least ten stories about it! It is interesting to remind yourself that everything you experience is simply a space/time event. It has no meaning until you assign one to it. That's where story comes in.

What do you notice when people create meaning for themselves through the events you are experiencing together? When you meet the spouse of a co-worker or someone else waiting for the bus, how do they appear to frame the stories they tell you? What does that tell you about the storylines they are living within? What does it say about *your* storylines? (Remember, this exercise is about *noticing,* not about judgement!)

Pay attention to the media. When you pick up a magazine or other publication, what do you notice about the story it is presenting? Any publication or broadcast is geared to a certain audience. It is designed around a particular storyline. Can you identify it? It is a very interesting thing to become conscious of the storylines in which you choose to participate.

Pay attention to the built environment — all the human-made structures around you. If you don't think you live inside a story, guess again. Our largest cities tell multiple stories, of how they grew, of how they wish to be seen, about what is considered important. Capital cities are the best example of this, but it is true for any town. Each of them has a story to convey. Your office space is no different. Pretend you've never been there before and take a look at it with fresh eyes. What story do you see? What about the restaurant or shop you're visiting? The online store? All of them are stories in action. What can you notice?

Try to discover your own storyline. Listen carefully to yourself. What stories are *you* sharing and why? What is your intention with sharing each story? Which ones are you consuming and why?

Being awake is not an easy thing. It is far easier to be habitual and simply float along. **But awareness is the first step towards choice.** *You've been given a challenge. Will you rise to it?*

> Stories travel across borders of all kinds. Which stories will you allow to live rent-free in your head?

It's all about the framing. Perhaps you've heard the phrase "the medium is the message." It is possible to have two different experiences of the same thing when it is framed in a different way. Researchers do that all the time. They frame a task, and ask the research subjects to do it. How they frame the task makes a huge difference to the outcome. Have a look at the TEDx talk by Nat Kendall-Taylor[4] about the science of framing and listen to how he talks about stories.

What do you want to explore about your own story or how story works?

Join the 365 ALIVE! Community and share the stories of your journey.
Find us on Facebook. Look for: "365 ALIVE! Community"

WEEK 3
Make a story health check

 *Think about...*

Make your own story health check this week.

Considering the stories you observed around you last week, which ones reflected a healthy environment? What did the stories say about how people see their well-being? Focus specifically on the kind of stories being shared in the community you live in or the place you work. What do they say about how people see their well-being? How "healthy" are these stories for the connection and respect between people? What story could you add to the mix that raises the level of health and well-being?

It's a fascinating thing to focus on health and take a look at its parameters. From a physical point of view, vitality of the body is an indicator of a person's health. All parts of the body need to be functioning well, separately and together, for high vitality. Over a period of time some parts can take up the slack for others, but over a longer period, this wears the system out.

From a permaculture point of view, the indicators of a healthy ecosystem are found in its boundary territories — a higher diversity in the boundaries of one area to another indicates a healthy ecosystem. A natural ecology that is more diverse in its boundary region is also more robust.

From humanity's point of view, stories are an indicator of the health and vitality of human systems. Are the prevailing stories based on lack, suspicion, control or fear? Or are they stories of possibilities, trying something out, hope, inclusion? What is the mix of positive and negative stories? What themes do you hear across stories? Which people feature in the stories? Who is telling them? How? Where? Whose stories get told and whose get listened to? How do groups of people show up (or not) and what are the prevailing stories asking us to know about them? For example, within your social group, has someone dropped away? What story is implied about that person in their presence or absence?

> Stories are an indicator of the health and vitality of human systems. Consider yourself a Story Archaeologist.

Take action...

Consider yourself a Story Archaeologist. Pretend you're about to enter a new tribe and learn about its way of operating. Take careful note of the stories that are told around you in the office, in the boardroom, in the bank, in the community, in the café, at the dinner table. What are you hearing? What kind of stories are people sharing? Is there a common thread or theme? Since stories provoke other stories, see if you can follow the thread as it moves from person to person. What is your overall sense of the kinds of stories alive in the places where you are right now?

Reflect on what this means. Consider the stories you've been listening to this week:

- **Who** told stories in the groups you were in? Whose stories were listened to and whose were not? Whose stories seemed to have more weight or importance? Why is that?
- **What** kind of stories did you hear? Were they intended to share experience? Reinforce a point of view? Direct something? Reflect or reject something?
- **How** were stories shared? Informally? As a presentation? Digitally? One to many or in a group? What was the impact of these different modes?
- Since stories are a reflection of **culture**, what kind of culture(s) have you been experiencing?
- Make a note in your journal about how this research has impacted you and what you now see as a result.

# Have a look...

Images and stories are closely linked. Our Western culture, driven by the internet, is becoming more and more image driven. It is said that a picture is worth a thousand words, but an image is a holder for the stories we place on it. It is also a carefully curated piece of reality.

Reflect for a moment on the movement of images through history around famous people. In the time of President Kennedy in the early 1960s, crowds who came to see him and other famous celebrities wanted autographs and often displayed them. A few decades later people wanted to take photos of their icons and the red carpet was full of flashbulbs. Now the most predominant form of image on the internet is the selfie.[5] What does that say about how our storylines are shifting? What does it say about our personal and societal health?

Images are used to provoke the senses and evoke emotion. What powerful images have you noticed lately and what stories do they bring up in you?

Stories are like a cup of tea.

Kindness is the gift of life.

THE MORE YOU STEEP IN THEM THE MORE TRUE THEY SEEM TO BE. WHAT STORY ARE **YOU** IN RIGHT NOW?

MARY ALICE ARTHUR

WEEK 4
What stories have you been steeping in?

Think about...

The stories surrounding us shape our present and also our future.

It is important to become aware of the story you're living in, because most likely it will be the story you are living into as well!

Stories have great power. First, stories are part of the way our neural network — our brain — is structured. We hold our memories and experiences in story form. That makes them easier to find, but it also means they are fluid. Memories can change over time, as anyone who watches crime dramas can attest.

Perhaps you are like me, wondering about specific memories. Were they experiences I really had, or were they told to me often enough that I came to see them as my own? Were they shaped by a picture I saw in the family photo album? Did it *really* happen?'

We can be easily swayed by someone who has a potent and strongly held story. Our story can also be changed if we hear another version of it repeatedly over time. Propaganda in any form is an example of this phenomenon.

Family and ethnic cultures also work like a cup of tea where stories are concerned. An oft-repeated story can be taken as true, unless another story

Stepping back from the prevailing stories of culture enables you to have a look and make an informed choice.

surfaces to change the perception. Each of us is a fabrication of the stories we hold about ourselves and the stories others hold about us. The same is true for societies and cultures. The stories might be true, and they are never the whole of who we are.

The same is true for stories we tell about other people. They — whoever they are — are so much more multidimensional and complex than one story can portray. Yet the human brain likes to simplify and lump things together in order to feel in control.

Our brains are geared to help us make quick decisions. This stems from an ancient human need for survival. In our hunter/gatherer days our brains were wired to make quick decisions to keep us safe.

Human culture can still act like this, making us less curious and more afraid of difference. Our brains evaluate others who are strangers to us in about three to five seconds — about the time it takes to decide whether you will pick up a hitchhiker or not.

What does it take to make the space for wiser choice? As a friend of mine[6] used to say: "You can't tell who's calling the tune when you stay on the dance floor. The only way to see the orchestra is from the balcony." The reason for stepping back from the prevailing stories of culture is to be able to get some distance, have a look and then make an informed choice.

Take action...

Go after a story and find out if it is really true. These days there are plenty of sound bites to choose from — short storylines that people pick up on social media feeds and send around to everyone on their list. These stories travel like wildfire, but often they are not the full story. They may not even be true. Take on the role of investigative journalist and probe. Ask others in your family about a story of which you know little. Research an inflammatory headline. Find more perspectives on the same event. There is always more than one side to a story.

What stories have you been steeping in? Begin making a list of the stories that have defined your life and how you see the world. What stories have you received from your family, ethnicity, race, culture, society, affiliations (like clubs, sports teams, hobby groups)? What stories have you received about your gender role, status, place in society, potential or future possibilities? What picture of the world has this given you? Is it the one you want to keep?

With so many sound bites and opinions flying around the world, it is easy to get stuck in simple stories about people, places and situations, rather than the nuanced and complex realities they reflect. Novelist Chimamanda Ngozi Adichie[7] reminds us of the danger of a single story in her brilliant TED talk.

PART TWO

Mapping Your Personal StoryField

When we experience something, our mind makes a story of it in order to make sense of it. From that story springs the meaning we make of it. Brain scientists tell us that we might not have memories at all, but that our stories become our memories. That means that a story acts as a filter or a lens on the world, coloring our perception of it and our actions in response. Can you catch the lenses your stories are creating?

At the same time, none of us lives within the frame of a single story — we are all StoryFields. We are the intersection of all the stories we hold about ourselves, all the stories we inhabit and also those that have co-opted us.

That means I might tell myself that I am an international citizen and have a global view of the world, but I am also looking at the world partially through the lens of where and how I grew up. I may have grown up in one place and now live somewhere else on the planet, in a different field of stories that give me a very different perspective of the world. Maybe I have a passport that says one thing, but I feel like that's not my identity. It may co-opt me anyway when someone notices my accent or makes an assumption about me based on what they think they see or know. *Hey, that's not me!* I call out in frustration.

But who am I? Who are you? Most often our stories live below the surface of our consciousness, calling the shots as we react to the world. If you want to move from reactor to creator, you need to uncover the stories on which your worldview is based. Becoming conscious of something is the first step towards changing it.

In Part 2 we will be working with your personal stories to see what they are, where they came from and how they were shaped. Gaining a new perspective on your personal StoryField gives you the choice about what story you want to live in now.

Climb mountains

not so the world can see you, but so
you can see the world.

DAVID MCCULLOUGH JR.

WEEK 5

How can stories help you take an eagle-eye view?

 *Think about...*

Sometimes you need an eagle-eye view, a moment to stand above it all to see the big picture.

A moment of total reorientation to my place in the world came when I stood at the rim of the Grand Canyon in Arizona. It was so huge that I felt almost like an ant on its shoulder. I stared down and was drawn into the many colors of stone. I marveled at the ages it must have taken water to carve away all that rock. I could sense timelessness and the overwhelming urge of life to create. That was a foundational change in my story of myself and nature. What would you see if you looked at your world from a different perspective?

Remember back to a time in childhood when you studied something smaller than yourself. Perhaps it was an insect in the grass, a small fish in a big tank, an unfolding flower or the inside of an alarm clock.

To the insect, you were a giant and the carpet of grass was a forest. To you, the insect and the leaves of grass were very small and part of a bigger picture. You were studying the small things in order to understand something bigger — the puzzle of how things fit together or maybe even shed light on the mystery of life itself.

We can create the same effect with stories. When I narrate my life from the inside *(Today I experienced)* then I'm at the center of my story; I can get stuck in the details. Think of any heated argument between people when the focus falls on exactly who did what. My life feels like a movie happening around me where I'm the main character and everyone else is merely a supporting actor. Maybe I'm even walking the dog to my own personal soundtrack! Every moment is another snapshot of reality, and they can feel quite separate to each other.

If I step back a bit and take a helicopter view, I can begin to see patterns. I can get a sense of flow. I can see how something back there influences something later on. I can begin to see the mosaic that has created the me I think I know.

Seen from the inside, life can be big and overwhelming. Seen from a different point of view, the "red thread"[8] can be found that links things together. The key is perspective.

Write your own fairytale. During this exercise, you're going to be writing your own real-life story, but in the form of a myth or fairytale, and in the third person. So instead of writing *I was born on …* you will be writing *She was born on …* or *It was a Tuesday when he….*

Writing in the third person makes it much easier to allow whatever unfolds in the story to simply unfold. You are *in* this story, but you can stand outside it at the same time. Doing it like this helps you see yourself in a totally new light.

Your job is simply to begin, listen deeply and see what unfolds when you follow the prompts below. Let whatever arises in your intuition guide you, rather than forcing something to happen. See what details offer themselves and write them into the story. What do things look like? Feel like? Sound like? The more you use the language of the senses, the more interesting and compelling your story will be, and the more clues it will give you about your interior life.

Is resistance coming up? Then there's surely something to learn from doing the exercise! Often the conscious mind doesn't want to see what has been below the surface, believing more in the challenge of discomfort than the possibility of a gift. Remind yourself that perfection is not required. All that is required is to *begin*.

Here are some prompts to help the story unfold:
- Once upon a time there was …
- S/he was given the gifts of …
- And also …
- And then …
- Finally s/he came to the crossroads called …
- Standing at the crossroads was …
- Who tells her/him that _____ must be left behind and _____ must be picked up now to move forward, and hands him/her a parchment which reads …

Give yourself spaciousness to really be with the story and see what comes. Dedicate some quiet time. Turn off the phone. Create a special space to sit in where you feel free to reflect.

If you have someone you trust, share your story with them and ask them to play the role of your journey partner, the one who is listening carefully for what's underneath, behind, and around the story and who can give you insights into the elements and unfolding of the story. Here are some things you might want them to comment on:
- What does your journey partner notice about your founding story and the stories that follow?
- What are the gifts you hold and how are you using them now?
- What do they notice about what happens at the crossroads and who is standing there?
- What is the significance of the name of the crossroads, and what is the name of the road you now need to take?

> Seen from the inside, life can be overwhelming. Seen from a different point of view, the "red thread" can link things together.

- What did you leave behind and what travels with you now? How is that significant?
- And then … What does your journey partner notice about your founding story and the stories that follow?

Let this work sink in and continue to move in you for a while. See what happens to your view of the world and your place in it. You may want to return at a later time and work with your story again.

Have a look…

The 1977 short movie *Powers of Ten*[9] takes us on a journey from a person lying in a park out into space and then back. Each time the scene changes we zoom out to the power of ten. We start out with the person in the middle of the frame and then see the whole park. Then we see the wider landmass, then the continent and eventually we are way out in space and the Earth is merely a dot in the cosmos. Then we turn around and make the journey all the way back. How different things look depends on how you look at them. What perspective does this give you?

My fairytale...

Post your fairytale in the *365 ALIVE!* Community and find others that speak to you

WEEK 6
What stories are shaping your stance in the world?

 *Think about...*

What story are you telling yourself right now about who you are and what is possible?

If you stop and come to stillness for a moment, you may hear that small voice in your head that's narrating your life. It tells you stories about the intentions of others. It talks to you about your performance (or lack of it). It creates stories about the meaning of each moment. How are these stories shaping your life and your stance in the world? What would you change if you could?

Sometimes, we are not in charge of life, our story is. Where does that story come from? Usually, it's a mosaic. Part comes from the upbringing we experienced. Perhaps you've heard a parent's voice in your head or even coming out of your mouth! Our family dynamics shape how we deal with close relationships, how we enter into intimacy, how safe it feels to make mistakes or try something new.

Another part of our story comes from our friendship and community circles. These relationships are the next circle of stories out from the core and play a key role in molding our behavior, especially in groups. Peers have a strong influence on how we see ourselves and what agency we believe we have to take action in the world.

Some of our foundation stories come from our societal context. We are flooded every day with stories from our culture and from the media, telling us who and what we should be. These stories give us messages about what gender is and what role it should play. They confirm whether we have "acceptable" beliefs or habits, or whether we are "the other," dangerous, powerless or powerful. For those fitting the dominant narrative, race, privilege and power become invisible. Everyone else has to work around these issues every day.

Many of these stories, the stories that have co-opted our own, form the internalized voices that become our inner critic.

Neuroscientist Jill Bolte Taylor[10] calls the negative voices the "Itty Bitty Shitty Committee," because they act like a gallery of critics that bring you down and wear you out. I call mine "The Movie Critic" and I picture him in an overstuffed armchair with a clipboard, rating the scene playing out in front of him with a giant red pencil. Giving your inner critic a persona helps make it easier to deal with. It makes it easier to say to it, *"Thanks for sharing, and I'm going to do this instead…."*

Making peace with your inner critic changes your storyline. You can't always change what happens to you. But you CAN change the story you tell yourself about it.

> We are flooded every day with stories telling us who we should be. Many of them form the internalized voice of our inner critic.

Get acquainted with your inner critic. Give them a persona, even a name. What does your inner critic look like? What is their highest intention? (I know mine is actually there to help me look for the best possible outcome in every situation; it's just the ultra-critical way he does it that isn't helpful!) Be aware that you may not have one critic, but an entire committee. That's okay. Let them speak to you and allow them to be heard. You don't have to take on the criticism, but understanding it more deeply will give you insight.

Try some free writing. Write down a question to your inner critic and then listen for the answer. Write that down too.

Flip your storyline. Pick out an incident or event in your life that you keep telling yourself a negative story about. What happens to your perception if you:

- Retell the story from your perspective with a different outcome?
- Tell the story from someone else's perspective or the perspective of an object or natural feature?
- Add, "… and then I learned … and as a result I…." What creative, positive or strengthening outcomes are produced as a result?

Take a look at a life story where choosing perception makes all the difference. The *New York Times* posted an item on physics teacher Jeffrey Wright[11]. He is positively on fire to help his high school students learn something. And he also wants them to know he cares. He shows up with intensity and a great love of learning, which encourages them to do the same. In his own life, he is inspired by a son with multiple handicaps, who daily teaches him what love is all about.

WEEK 7
What stories are you living up to?

Think about...

Each of us is living up to the stories we hold.

What stories inspired you as a child? Which influenced how you saw the world or your place in it? How are these stories impacting you today?

Do you remember the stories you loved most as a child? I remember the book I loved the most had a bright red cover. The story was about a little girl and her many older brothers living in Chinatown in San Francisco. Many years later the red makes sense to me because this red is the color of Chinese New Year and that was the time of year in which the story was set.

Why did I love that book so much? I didn't grow up in a big city, I grew up surrounded by corn fields. Was it because she was the smallest and all the brothers took care of her? (I was the oldest child and had two younger sisters.) Was it because of the bright pictures and the holiday theme? I asked for it again and again.

Even now, I'm not sure why I wanted to hear it so many times. But I think it was the strong sense of community this story conveyed that made me love it. I still aspire to create community. Stories like this encouraged me to become an avid reader, and I traveled the world between the covers of my books before I went out there for real.

Later I was given the book *Momo*, by Michael Ende, and it is still one of my favorite stories of all time. I like to say I met Momo when I was twenty and she was twelve. She's still twelve, but has remained my lifetime role model for listening.

Perhaps your favorite story was one told in your family or community. Or maybe one your parents or siblings made up. Or one you heard at a summer camp or school. Maybe *Harry Potter* changed your life. Your favorite stories may have nothing to do with home, but everything to do with you!

Where did you find stories when you were younger? What did those stories teach you about life and about who you could be or wanted to be? What have you carried with you from the stories of your younger days?

When we played as children, we embodied stories in order to try them on for size. As adults, sometimes we can get stuck inside our stories. Remember, a role is just a story you've decided to carry for a while. It may be appropriate to keep carrying it or it may be time to put it down.

Take action...

> What did stories teach you about life and about who you wanted to be? We embody stories in order to try them on for size.

Find and reread or retell a story from your childhood.
- What made this story so special for you?
- What echoes can you notice from that story to now? How did the story influence how you saw the world?
- How does this story still speak to you?
- What has changed in how you see the story now?

Imagine a character from that story as a friend, mentor or traveling companion. Where would you go or what would you do with your friend? What might be possible because they are with you? What quality or qualities do they embody that you'd like to have? Invite your friend to be alongside you during the coming week and give you feedback or advice. What perspectives can they share about your experiences?

 *Have a look...*

Pick a few stories to listen to. There are many collections online. One of my favorites is **Story Online**, featuring well-known actors reading children's books. First, Hector Elizondo reading *Somebody Loves You, Mr. Hatch*. And then, because his voice is just too good to miss, James Earl Jones reading *To Be a Drum*[12].

> **The happening and telling are very different things.**
>
> This doesn't mean that the story isn't true, only that I honestly don't know anymore if I really remember it or only remember how to tell it. Language does this to our memories, simplifies, solidifies, codifies, mummifies.
>
> **An oft-told story is like a photograph in a family album.** Eventually it replaces the moment it was meant to capture.
>
> KAREN JOY FOWLER
> "WE ARE ALL COMPLETELY BESIDE OURSELVES"

WEEK 8

How are your stories shaping your memories?

 *Think about...*

From our brain's point of view, stories *are* our memories.

We don't hold on to the event and its factual experience, as much as we keep the meaning we've made of an event. Stories help us store what matters to us, but that means each of us will see things in a different way. There is more than a grain of truth in the old saying: *There are many sides to a single story.*

I have a sister with a technicolor memory. She will often regale us with some memories which take me completely by surprise. She talks about people, places and things with a great amount of color, life and detail. Sometimes I ask her if I was there too, because I don't remember it like that, or even at all.

Then there are some of my own memories that make me wonder. Are they real? I think they came from family photos or oft-told stories. They exist like snapshots in my mind, as if frozen in time. Or they are only a fragment — I can see the door to the house, but I don't know how to find the road that leads to the door.

Telling the same story again and again can force it to hold a certain shape, like an insect stuck in amber. We assign a meaning to an event and then polish that meaning. It's almost like polishing a stone so it's shiny and ready to share with someone else. After a while, we don't look at other possible meanings.

We lose the ability to look at the story from a different perspective or point of view.

With the advent of technology, two things are becoming highly impacted: our ability to observe details, and our imagination. Both of these are key qualities for storytellers.

The brain loves to fill in the blanks. So imagine us sitting together and me telling you: *Yesterday I went through the park with my dog running alongside.* What kind of dog would you picture? What does the park look like?

If you want me to see more exactly what you are picturing in your mind, first imagine it vividly, with all the detail you can manage. Then, **tell me about it.** Details help bring a story to life, and only through imagination can our stories reach others. Practicing both of these will make you a better story listener and a better storyteller.

Try an experiment. When you next have a group experience this week — like a meeting, a conference, a party or a family dinner — invite two or three others to share their stories of the event afterwards. How are they different to what you experienced? Imagine these stories are the facets of a diamond, each helping to make the diamond more real, more three dimensional. What can you learn about your own patterns of noticing?

Take some time reviewing old memories. Think about a time when you were experiencing something you enjoyed — perhaps a creative meeting or a holiday or adventure. Go into that memory and see how much detail you can bring into your imagination. If you're someone who likes journaling, make yourself some notes. What can you see, sense, touch, taste, smell in this experience? Where can you shift your focus, almost like a film director pointing the camera in a new angle? What changes about the memory as a result?

Check your powers of observation. Take some time to be alert, awake and aware. If you've ever read or seen the stories about the famous detective Sherlock Holmes you know he had an ultra-keen eye for details. What can you observe when you are next on public transport, or walking through a crowded space? What can you take in if you really pay attention? How easy is it to stay focused? What have you learned about yourself as a result?

Memories are fascinating things. You'll learn a lot by simply asking an older relative to share some of their memories or by asking people to tell about a photo you have. The Rescued Film Project[13] helps to find and restore photographic memories. One of the stories you can watch is about memories captured more than 70 years ago on film and only just seen for the first time.

> Details bring a story to life, and only through imagination can our stories reach others. Practicing both will make you a better storyteller.

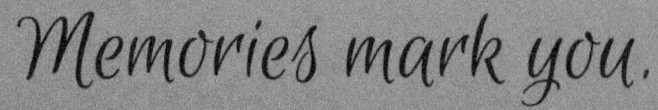

Memories mark you.

Moments in time that cast a shadow over your life and change you forever. Remembering is to relive – to be in the same moment all over again.

LAURIE LEE, "CIDER WITH ROSIE"

WEEK 9
What stories do you want to relive?

Think about...

***Cider with Rosie*[14] is Laurie Lee's much-beloved memoir of growing up in the UK countryside.**

His family didn't have much, but he had a mother who loved her children deeply and encouraged their imaginations. His memories enabled readers to touch the experience of a close-knit family, childhood adventures, joy and tragedy. What memories do you want to relive?

All of us have had times when we experienced the beauty and abundance of the world, whether it was for a moment or a longer time. We have experienced times of challenge that led to learning. We've had times of grief and times of joy. We've had people who helped us to see the world or ourselves differently.

Remembering these moments can be like finding a gemstone at the edge of a rocky path. They stay in our memories, casting light that can help dispel shadows. They can give us an anchor point when it seems that life has cast us into the sea and we've drifted very far from shore.

Taking a walk down memory lane to retrieve some of these stories reinvigorates the present moment. Yet so many of us get stuck in the day-to-day minutiae, ride home wrapped up in technology, and then go to sleep in the in-tray. We are trapped into living forward at such a pace that our past drains the future instead of vitalizing it. Worried about tomorrow, we dwell on memories that pull us down — failures, near misses, regrets, irritations, hurt and blame.

Remembering where we, and life, were at our best gives us more courage and resilience. Remembering stories that support us, help us to be vulnerable, and touch us in the heart and spirit restores our balance in a troubled world. They remind us that we — and life — are valuable and have gifts to share.

Since memories are physical as well as mental, we can remind ourselves — on a cellular level — what we felt and what we did in those valued moments. This is more than simply retrieving a memory; it is *embodying* a memory and the possibility of a different future. Our stories give us the keys to recreate those experiences.

> **Remembering where we were at our best gives us more courage and resilience. It restores balance in a troubled world.**

Take action...

Find a place and time where you have the space to be quietly with yourself or with someone else. Ask your partner, or yourself, these questions and make some notes about the stories you tell in response. What was happening? What role did you play?

- Take us to a moment when you felt confident and sure of yourself or a moment when a difficult situation came to a happy resolution and you were a key part of it.
- What experience have you had where you felt close to someone else, or deeply understood, or part of a family? Tell the story about it.
- Tell about a time of challenge or tragedy which strengthened or enlightened you.
- Tell about a moment when you felt deeply at home.
- When was a moment you felt part of nature or totally natural?
- Recount one of your happiest moments.
- *Invent your own prompts …*

Have a look at what you captured from your stories.

- What can you see about your skills, talents, actions, behaviors from these stories? *What were you doing?*
- What can you tell about your attitude, focus, worldview, inner self, values from these stories? *Who were you being?*
- What have you learned about yourself and what can you put into place to create more skillfulness, courage and resilience now?

Stories can save your life! Upworthy reported about a mother who wrote to *Harry Potter* author J.K. Rowling about her premature daughter, Juniper[15]. It was touch and go whether the small baby would live. But her family began to read the books out loud to her and she seemed to respond. Indeed, she began to thrive. There's something magical about how much stories can influence us!

Your whole life and

the Story of your journey

is the landscape picture on the front of the box of a 1,000 piece puzzle. The pieces are each a small sticky note that ends in mid-sentence. You simply need to figure out where each one starts and ends.

ASHLY LORENZANA

WEEK 10
How can stories help you understand life?

 *Think about...*

Sometimes, life only makes sense in retrospect.

Have you ever found yourself wanting to stand in the middle of it all, throw your hands up to the sky and shout: *"What's it all mean?!?"* It can be years later that the pieces fall into place and you begin to understand your life journey. That's why they say that hindsight is 20/20 and that life is lived forward but only understood looking back. *What part of your story has made sense recently and why?*

Perhaps stories were invented to help us get a grip on life.

Usually life is like a river, constantly flowing and never stopping. It skips along like water rushing merrily over stones. Sometimes it becomes a rushing torrent, dragging you along with it, out of control and hanging on for dear life. At times you find yourself spinning in an eddy. Where's it all going?

A story, though, is like a snapshot in time. It is a moment that has a beginning, a middle and an end. Because of this construction, a few things can happen. First, there is a bounded moment to study. We know when it starts, we can examine the action, we know when it ends. We don't have to make sense of everything at once, we are just looking at a particular episode in a longer drama.

Second, because of this time restriction, we find it easier to step into the shoes of the characters in the story. We can study their motivation, follow the turn of events and see how the action plays out. We try it on for size, imagining what it would be like to be like them, or act like them. If we're looking at our own story, we can take time to examine our own motivation, see what our actions led to and how we felt in response. This is where some of our greatest learning can take place.

We are less distracted by what came before (glossed over in that phrase "once upon a time" or "once there was") or what comes after ("then they lived happily ever after" or "she's alive and well and living in New Zealand"). And because this is something that already happened, we can string the pieces together and make a story of it, which is what the brain automatically tries to do, in order to first make sense, and then later make meaning, of what happened.

Sometimes it takes a long enough arc of time — and the willingness — to look back and make sense. In another point in time in your life you will have grown both the distance and more life experience to take a fundamentally different look at your story. Remember, a story is not forever frozen in a particular shape. The sense you make of it, what you decide to allow to play out in your life, can change. What the story means is up to you.

> The sense you make, what you decide to allow to play out in your life, can change. What the story means is up to you.

Take action...

Take the helicopter view of your life. Decide, for the moment, to be curious and intrigued. Draw a circle on a piece of paper and draw three lines across it as if you were cutting up six equal pieces of pie. For each of these "slices" think of a defining moment in your life, a moment when your life was changed. It doesn't have to be a dramatic or intense moment; it might have been a small moment that later had a very big effect. Or perhaps a moment that really stays in your memory, but you don't know why. These can be thought of as "turning points," where your story turned in a new direction.

Looking back over these moments more closely, what made no sense at the time, that makes sense now? What do you now understand that you didn't in the moment? Where can you see how one thing led into another to get you to where you are today?

What are you grateful for as a result?

Where is the story going from here? Cast your mind forward. If you keep on telling the story as you have been, things will probably stay the same. Is that good news? Where do you want your story to go from here?

Take a look around you. Have a deeper look at the photos you have, the things you've brought into your space, the memorabilia you have collected. What stories do they represent? What do the different things mean to you now? How do these things string together in the bigger puzzle of your life?

> *A story should have a beginning, a middle and an end, but not necessarily in that order.*
>
> — JEAN-LUC GODARD

WEEK 11
Where are your beginnings, middles and endings right now?

 *Think about…*

We often think of stories in terms of literature or movies. Everything tidy and wrapped up within the frame of the covers of the book or the length of the movie. But life doesn't usually flow like that.

There are things ending and things beginning and things in the messy middle, all at the same time. That can make it confusing. Where are your beginnings, middles and endings right now?

It could be said that life is like an ecosystem, a forest or a river system perhaps. In the South Island of New Zealand there are **braided rivers** (and if you look up "braided river images" on the internet you'll see plenty!). Braided rivers happen in landscapes with a wide riverbed. They appear to be many rivers meandering across the landscape, criss-crossing each other as they flow.

They aren't really separate rivers, but separate streams of the same river. Each river carries water from the main stream, but also what it collects in its own flow. This means that a single braided river touches much more landscape than an ordinary river. Our life stories are like that too.

In different parts of our lives, different parts of our stories are interacting. At home you may be in a long-term relationship that has spanned years. You are in the middle of this story. Perhaps you've had a child recently. A new chapter has begun, but is weaving into a current storyline.

Perhaps at work you've joined a new organization, a new story. Maybe you've decided to stop being part of a group you used to enjoy. Or someone you know is at the end of life. The story is finishing here. And perhaps somewhere else there is conflict and breakdown, you are in the messy middle unsure of where it all will go now.

Often conflict between people and groups happens when we believe that we are in one part of the story and others think we are in a different place. When organizations try to implement culture change, you can clearly see this in action. Leaders of the organization may believe that everyone should be ready for change, but someone far away from head office may not even realize that change is coming. This is why it can feel as if there is so much friction and drag in change efforts — we all believe that we are at different parts of the story, or not even in the same story at all!

The key to staying afloat in all these stories in action is to become conscious of them and take a look at what stage they are in.

Take a look at your life in this moment at work, at home, in your community. What are the stories in play?

- *What stories are ending?* Where do you need to make a conscious closure? How could you honor the journey that is ending now? How can you mark the ending? What does conscious closure look like for you?
- *What stories are beginning?* How can you make an intentional start? How can you take time to make some reflection points early on? How do you want to mark this beginning?

- *What stories are in the messy middle?* What would help you to get some overview or eagle-eye perspective? How can you step out so you can step back in with a sense of clarity? How can you tend to yourself and others at this stage in the story? Where do you need greater awareness, skill or tact with what is unfolding?
- *Where do you sense new stories will arise?* Where do you sense a change or evolution coming? What will that require from you?

 Have a look...

We tend to think of life as an ongoing story. But what if it were possible to jump forward and rewind back to live some part again? The British movie *About Time* tells the story of male family members who can jump backwards in time. And a little video called *A Single Life*[16] takes a humorous look at the way life runs forward, backward and in all directions.

> Often conflict happens when we believe that we are in one part of the story and others think we are in a different place.

Every *Story* has an inbreath and an outbreath.
The important thing is to keep breathing.

MARY ALICE ARTHUR

WEEK 12
Which of your stories needs to breathe?

 *Think about...*

Breath is so intrinsic to life that we don't even think about it.

But it is a powerful tool. If you breathe deeply you stay calmer, you have more access to imagination and curiosity. You are more present. You have the ability to respond, rather than react. You have gained a moment to be in charge of your story, rather than your story being in charge of you. *Where can focusing on your breathing this week help you?*

Mostly people don't pay attention to their breath. It just happens naturally. The body is set up to take care of this function, as it takes care of so many others. But **pay attention.** Right now! How are you breathing?

Is your breath shallow? Rapid? Are you breathing only into the top of your lungs or all the way down to your stomach? Become conscious of the air as it passes through your nose and into your lungs.

Every breath has four parts. The inhale, the briefest of pauses at the top of the breath, the exhale and a moment of pause at the end. See if you can notice these four movements. Your body has learned to do this seamlessly.

The importance of noticing your breath is that it keeps you present. It keeps you grounded. Things may be happening around you, but you don't fly off somewhere in your thoughts and into old storylines if you keep paying attention. You have the possibility of responding with curiosity rather than emotion, to choose your reaction. You can choose what story you think you're in.

Breath is oxygenating your blood, which is pumping around your body. Without air, you would not be the living, breathing storyteller you are! Air is as necessary to the body as stories are to the human being.

Stories have their own in-and-out breath. And every story has movement — in, hold for a moment, out, reflect. Stories also need breathing space. They need animation. When we get stuck in our stories, stories also get stuck. Life is about movement. *Remember to keep breathing.*

 Take action...

> When you breathe, you gain a moment to be in charge of your story, rather than your story being in charge of you.

Are you in a story where you've forgotten to breathe? Reflect for a moment about the stories surrounding you. Is there something you're worrying about? Is there something you are hesitating to face? Maybe you need to breathe in to give yourself some courage and grounding to move forward. Maybe you are holding your breath and trying to keep a story under control or still. Maybe you need to breathe out. Where is breath needed in your storyline?

Is there somewhere your story is out of breath? A place where many of us experience being stuck is in our family of origin. We know we've grown up and moved on, and yet we seem to be stuck in the same familiar story and repeating patterns when we get around our family again. Find a place in one of your stories where you feel stuck and craft a few alternative ways the story could unfold.

Have a look at them. Which one seems the most outlandish to you? Which one the most likely? Which one would you prefer?

Allow yourself to play with this story and with the alternative scenarios throughout the coming week. Stay curious to what might unfold. What happens?

Becoming aware of your breath is a good place to start. In her online video, psychologist and author of *Breathe*, Dr. Belisa Vranich[17] explains a breathing technique that will calm you down, even in the most stressful of situations.

The 1980 film *Ordinary People* portrays a family in the midst of a stuck story. In the aftermath of a boating accident, which took the life of the much-loved older brother, the younger son swings between guilt and suicide. Finally he begins the healing process, supported by his father. His mother, on the other hand, remains in isolation, so stuck in her story that she cannot change. It is a powerful mirror of what happens when stories get stuck and when stories shift.

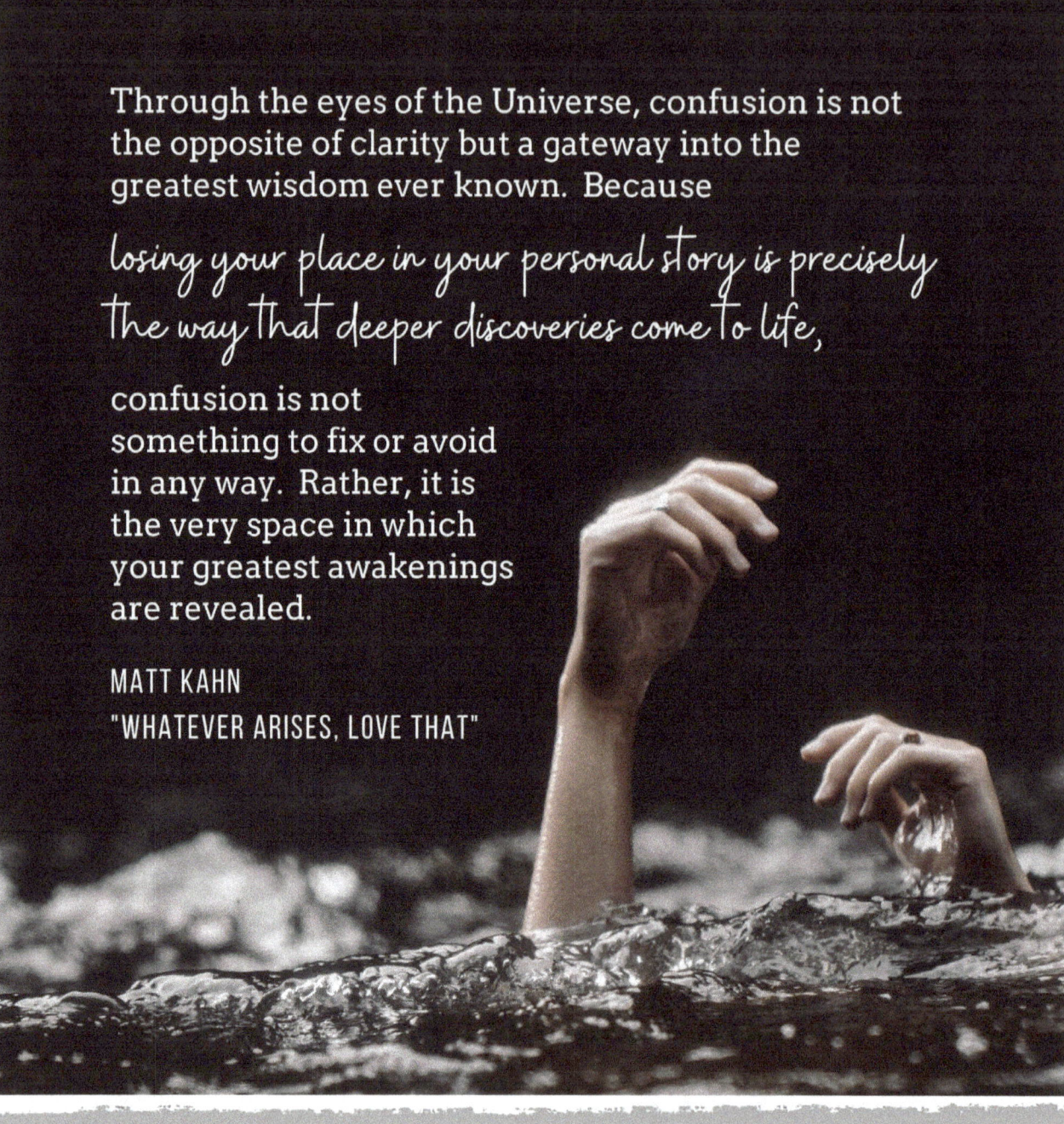

Through the eyes of the Universe, confusion is not the opposite of clarity but a gateway into the greatest wisdom ever known. Because

losing your place in your personal story is precisely the way that deeper discoveries come to life,

confusion is not something to fix or avoid in any way. Rather, it is the very space in which your greatest awakenings are revealed.

MATT KAHN
"WHATEVER ARISES, LOVE THAT"

WEEK 13

How is "not-knowing" offering you a new view of your story?

 *Think about...*

Being in confusion is decidedly uncomfortable.

As humans, we don't like it very much. It feels *messy*, even downright dangerous. It can make us feel lost and afraid. But the not-knowing is also a generative place, a place where the new can come forth. If you can stay there for a moment, you might just discover something. What do you need to do to grow your capacity to stay in the not-knowing?

Everyone knows that feeling — that sense of standing in the fog, not seeing anything clearly. You feel as if you've taken a step past the end of your known map of the world. Issues are piling up as complexity rises from ankle deep to waist high and you don't know what to do. It feels like you've fallen into a hole. **Welcome to the not-knowing.**

Yes, this is an actual place. We all hit it sooner or later. Your project gets cancelled or you're suddenly moved to a new team. A relationship stagnates. The dream you had for your life dries up. Someone dies. The long-seething tension in the community is about ready to explode and people are looking to you for answers.

For most of us, the overwhelm of no clear direction feels so uncomfortable that we immediately try to find a way out. When we are alone we distract ourselves with action — we want to *do* something, *anything!* — or we numb ourselves with our favorite addictions. Within organizational structures we often plan another meeting or ask for another report, or in some way try to deflect the fact that we don't know or there is no easy answer.

One reason the not-knowing is so frightening is that there is no proven way out of it. There's no best practice or process manual offering the answer. You have to find your own path. *But you do have a map.*

> When there is no clear way out of the not-knowing, it is a natural thing for humans to turn to stories.

When there is no clear way out of the not-knowing, it is a natural thing for humans to turn to stories. We share stories of similar times. We look to stories from people we admire. We take inspiration from adventurers or heroes. We remind each other of the times when we made it through adversity and we learn from each other's actions and success. **What stories are you holding that can help you stay in the not-knowing and find the treasure there?**

Take action...

Turn to your own stories. Think back to a time when you felt great confusion or you felt you'd lost your way. Perhaps it was a time when something ended suddenly or you felt somehow lost between this current moment and what should come next, or you were unsure if the dream you were holding was the right one. What did you learn from that time that can help you now, or the next time you feel confused or lost? See if you can find one or two more life stories and dig into them to find out what you already know about the not-knowing.

Listen to the stories of others. An invitation to others to share stories will create learning experiences and build relationships. Who can you ask? Is there someone in your circle you'd like to get to know better? This is a good way to start.

How can you make friends with the not-knowing? One way to relax is to assume you are amongst friends. How could the not-knowing be a friend to you at this time? How can you rest in this space, instead of trying frantically to be somewhere else? What happens if you turn toward it and really focus here? Try acting as if the not-knowing has come to be supportive and help you find a breakthrough. What happens if you decide to see it this way?

 *Have a look...*

Have a look at Adam Driver's story[18] of being in the not-knowing.
Adam Driver has had two significant times of not knowing what to do. At 17 this experience led him to the military. And later it led him to becoming a celebrated actor. His TED talk tells the story of what happened.

There's some real dark days where you just feel like the *Story* is falling apart in everyone. Just keep moving forward, even when you are bluffing, even when you don't quite know what is going to *happen next.*

— DAN SCANLON

WEEK 14

What movement could make all the difference to your story?

 *Think about...*

Movement is a good thing.

Not the "keep moving so it won't catch up with me" kind, but the kind of movement that keeps you flexible, warmed up, curious about what might come next, awake. Some people run, some dance, some travel in their imagination, some explore the edges in conversations with friends. What movement do you need this week?

The older you get, the more people tell you, "move it or lose it." It seems that muscles have a memory. It pays to remind them that they can move in a certain way as you age. Things like balance, strength, resilience and stamina are a matter of practice as much as they are a matter of ability.

The same is true when you think about possibility. When you were very young, you thought anything was possible. You loved stories of adventure and magic (well, maybe you *still* do!). But as you get older, reality hits and you most likely traded adventure for habit without realizing it. For so many, as they age, their world begins to shrink. And so does their story.

I remember one wintry November as an exchange student at the university in Hamburg, Germany. The town was cold, gray and rainy. The cement buildings perfectly matched the steel color of the sky. Everyone else on the floor in my student dormitory was away on holiday and the place echoed with the lack of their voices. I didn't have the money to go anywhere. I felt abandoned and got mightily depressed.

Pretty soon the door to my single room became the boundary. I turned inwards, but it wasn't very cheery there. My mood spiraled down even more. You might say, I got into the drainpipe and started polishing the sides.

It was only much later when I realized I never went to another floor to look for other people. I never went out to see what adventure might befall me. I let my world become small and depressed. I decided to be in the story of lack and stay there.

Movement of any kind would have helped. Writing, making music, walking, dancing, singing. Any of these would have given me the energy to make a move in my life. Stories are all about movement and in that moment, I allowed my story to get stuck. Physical, mental or emotional movement would have helped my story to move too.

Take action...

Where have you fallen into habit? For one day, really pay attention to what you do. What is your morning routine? How do you interact with your family? How do you get to work or if you work from home, what is your habit around it? Are there places you routinely go? Don't change anything; just notice.

Is there somewhere your story is falling apart? If this story seems broken beyond repair or is over, what do you choose instead? Would you most like to be graceful instead of awkward? Peaceful instead of upset? Forgiving instead of vindictive? Hopeful instead of hopeless?

Pretend for a moment you are a character in a story and script some new behavior for yourself. How would the you in the story act? Then try it on. **Act as if** for the rest of this week. See what happens.

Make a new move. Do something different this week. Go to a restaurant you've never been to before. Drive a different way to work or walk in a new direction. Do your morning routine in a different order. Speak to someone totally different than you. What opens up as a result?

 Have a look...

… at the movement around you. Take some time to observe and reflect on the movement taking place in your environment. You might want to hold the image of a time-lapse photography film in your mind. Movements so tiny that they don't seem to be happening make up the dramatic opening of flowers or the blur of people moving in Times Square in New York. If you stay very, very still, what movement do you notice around you? In you?

> Stories are all about movement. Physical, mental or emotional movement helps stories to move too.

WEEK 15
What will you decide to make out of what happened to you?

 Think about...

If everything were perfect, there would be nothing to dream about, nothing to work for, and nothing to challenge us.

In fact, there would be no growth at all. It is in your imperfections that the greatest learning can occur. Which imperfections, in yourself or others, can you love into acceptance or even transformation?

The best stories are never about perfect characters. They wouldn't be any good if they were. We love stories about imperfection and challenge because that makes them interesting. We want to know what will happen. We long to find out how the character will cope and in what ways the challenges or changes they face will transform them.

One reason for this is that we are primed to home in on someone else's motivation. From the moment we meet a new person in our life or a new character in a story, our minds are at work, trying to decide if we can understand their motivation. Is this a good guy who might have a secret in his past or a bad guy who deep down wants to be a hero? Is this a woman who will stay silent or decide to have courage and follow her heart, or a child who will learn to stand up to a bully?

We pay attention to their actions because this gives us an indicator of their feelings, and beneath that, the story they are living in and where it might go from here. It is the arc of the story that's important. That's why so many millions followed a small boy called Harry Potter all the way from his bedroom under the stairs to fulfilling his destiny.

Challenges and changes have come your way too. The important thing isn't that they happened, but what you made of them. What meaning did you make of what happened to you? How did you allow it to change your identity?

Each of those things you experienced is a facet of your character today. Good and bad don't matter so much, nor does the meaning you made at the time. You can make new sense and meaning now, from the vantage point of your older, wiser self, the one who wants to take charge of your story.

The event happened. You can't change that. But you *can* change what you decide to do with it.

 Take action...

> The event happened. You can't change that. But you can change what you decide to do with it.

What would you say are your imperfections? Everyone has them! As many spiritual teachers have reminded us in the past, if you think you are enlightened, just try being around your family! Please remember, this is not a time for judgement or blame, but a time for honest reflection. Maybe you can't quite believe in yourself or you think you are greedy or you've been told you're arrogant or aloof. If you were a character in a book, these attributes would make you more interesting, more *human*. As it is, you are a character in your own story, so the purpose of this exercise is to notice what material you have to work with and to decide where you want to go with it.

Draw a roadmap of your life up to now. Pretend your life has been a journey and sketch out a map of the road you've been on. You might want to put a marker at places where something significant happened, as road markings are made at the scene of an accident, or a plaque beside the road marks a place of historical interest. Did you get stuck in a ditch or in a water trap? Maybe there were places where the road was torn up, or something had fallen across it. Maybe there were detours or construction or the road disappeared. Maybe the terrain was steep and rocky or the road took many twists and turns.

You don't have to be an artist, but sketching it out, giving it a 3-D aspect, will help you to see more. Once you've finished, you might want to go back and note down who else was with you at the time and what meaning you made of each event. What do you see now as a result? Which stories have led you to be the person you are today?

Look for the red thread. Have a look at your roadmap. What were the most significant events for you, the ones that shape how you see life? Is there a series of events that hangs together to reinforce meaning or identity? How did these events become connected in your mind? Where did your imperfections turn out to be something else?

Reviewing all of the above, what do you see and what changes do you want to make now in your own storyline?

Make meaning and identity. Andrew Solomon[19] has made a career of writing about hardships. As a gay man, he lived through many of his own. In his TED talk, he describes how the worst moments of our lives are important — they make us who we are.

WEEK 16

Is your life telling the story you want to tell?

Think about...

If you look at your life as a story, with you as the central character, what kind of story is it?

A comedy? A tragedy? An action thriller? An adventure or a saga? Is it about little fights big? Underdog makes good? Still trying to find justice? I've got everything, what now? What story is your life telling? Is that the one you want to be living in?

Some of us live in technicolor. And some of us feel as if we're living in the black-and-white world of the 1927 silent movie *Metropolis*, working like cogs in a wheel. Some of us are the stars of a thriller and others are action heroes. And then there are those of us living road movies, taking in life and learning while on the journey from here to there, never quite finding home.

Some of us spend our lives inside a Cinderella look-alike story, not quite getting to the ball while the ugly stepsisters seem to walk away with all the treats. Others would love to show up in a romantic comedy, but face disappointment instead. In the movie *27 Dresses*, the main character is a bridesmaid again and again, always seeming to play the role of the superbly organized friend who takes care of everything, but never seems to walk down the aisle herself. One reason for this is that *she* thinks that's the story she's living.

It is fair to say that most of us are the heroes of our own story. We are the central character and everything happens around or to us. But some of us have something else as the focus. We are always in the supporting role to someone, or something, else. And if you are not in the center of your picture, who is? In fact, are you relegated to being a minor character or not showing up in your own story at all?

The main question here: *What story is your life telling? And is it the one you want to tell?*

What story is your life telling? And is it the one you want to tell?

 Take action...

If your life were a book ... Think about your life story as a book and consider these questions:

- *What are the chapters?* Write the heading like a Dickens novel: *"Chapter 3: in which she realizes she has outgrown the village and must make her way in a different world"* and make a few notes about what's in the chapter.
- *What are the parts of the book?* If you would group the chapters together into different parts, how would you group them? What do the parts represent?
- *What is the title?* Look at all the parts of this book of your life. What is it called?
- *Write a short introduction.* Pretend you are writing it from the vantage of a friend or colleague (who might be fictional), someone who knows you well and can help a reader to approach your life story.
- *Write an epilogue.* What happens from here or what do you hope for, having seen your life in this way?

Whose story reflects or sheds life on yours? Whose story reflects something to you about your own life? It might be that you are already aware of such a story or that you will keep your eyes and ears open this week to see what story arrives to fill this role.

 *Have a look...*

What is the art of being yourself? In her TED talk, Caroline McHugh[20] takes a look at why being more of yourself is what life is all about. She says successful individuals are those who figure out the unique gift the universe gave them when they incarnated.

Most of the pain we feel is nothing more than a *Story* that needs telling.

ASHLY LORENZANA

WEEK 17
What pain needs its story told?

Think about...

There seems to be a lot of pain being expressed in the world at present and it all finds a home in social media.

Conflicts are rife, challenges seem insurmountable and as over-connected people, we often feel overloaded with suffering on every level. The "out there" is suddenly "in here" too. We feel directly connected to human and ecological disasters half a world away. Or perhaps the pandemic or crisis is right outside the door. Heartache turns to heartbreak. It is hard not to be swept away by this overwhelming deluge of distressing information or have your own pain triggered.

Facing pain is a challenging thing. Most often we want to turn away from it either by distracting or medicating ourselves. We want it to turn it off, be rid of it, make it go away. Some people try to get rid of it by pushing it onto others and some bury it by pushing it down in themselves or trying to run away.

When it is not addressed, emotional pain can manifest in many ways — as physical symptoms, in strange behavior, in broken relationships or growing isolation. It can turn your own story from hopeful to hopeless.

But pain points to something. It has an underlying cause that is asking to be seen and dealt with. Pain can be the symptom of a deeper story longing for expression.

Perhaps there was a time when you didn't feel seen or appreciated. Or a time when the uniqueness you carry was seen as too different or not appropriate. Maybe your gifts took a long time to show themselves or were not able to be expressed. Perhaps a tender part of you was traumatized and you had to be strong and look like you didn't care in order to survive.

The Netflix series (and the original comic book) *The Umbrella Academy* picks up all these themes. Having a family doesn't mean you will know you are loved. Having powers doesn't mean you know how to wield them well. Being trained as a team doesn't mean you'll always feel part of one. Being told you need to rise to your destiny doesn't necessarily mean you'll know how to do it. And sometimes you'll feel trapped in a body that seems alien in a world you don't recognize, just longing for home.

Many experiences in life can cause a wounding. If it is not dealt with, also continued pain. This pain can be repeatedly triggered. A story suppressed can grow stagnant and toxic. A story expressed can shift and change. Where is there pain within *you* that needs expression?

Reflect on your life. Where is there pain calling for attention? Of course, this calls for courage and self-reflection. It may also call for support, so if you can, ask for help from someone trustworthy close to you. Don't turn away, but decide to turn towards the pain and see it for what it is: a part of your story. What stories is the pain tied to?

Decide to express your story. This doesn't mean you have to immediately tell someone else, but if you do, choose someone you trust. If you decide not to tell it, how could you make an expression that gives your story room to breathe? Can you write some of it? Draw it or make an artistic expression?

Build or create something? Dance it or find a song that expresses some of it and move to that? What is a safe way for you to open the lid — just a little — and allow the story to begin to move?

 Have a look...

There are no words in this story, but in the short film *Robot & Scarecrow*[21], two very different beings find each other, extend empathy and move through their pain. They profoundly impact each other as a result.

> Pain points to something. It can be the symptom of a deeper story longing for expression.

WEEK 18

What are the truthful stories that need to be shared now?

 **Think about...**

Have you heard of a fish story?

That's the story someone tells you about the fish they caught, except that each time they tell the story, the fish gets bigger and bigger — and usually the person gets more and more heroic. For all you know it might have been a whale and they were lucky to get away with their life! American writer Mark Twain had quite a sense of humor, but he also makes a good point. Where is honesty a better policy in your life? Where are your stories stretching the truth?

We all know that memory is selective. Stories are selective too! What you leave out is as important as what you include in a story, and sometimes more so. What you don't say leaves it up to the listener's imagination, just as what you describe makes it more tangible. What you leave out allows the light to shine on what's left. What remains becomes prominent, even a point of focus.

Sometimes, for the sake of making a story more interesting or exciting, the truth gets stretched. Any movie with the words "based on a true story" at the beginning is a case in point. I guess if Julia Roberts is going to play you (as she did a real-life woman in *Eat, Pray, Love* or earlier in *Erin Brockovich*) and the movie is intended for entertainment, some things might get changed. After all, there are many parts of life that are boring or repetitive; just ask any child who has been scolded for not making the bed.

There are countless little moments that go into making someone an overnight success. Thousands of hours go into making anyone a master of their craft. Music experts say part of what made the Beatles such a tight team musically were the six weeks playing every night in Hamburg clubs fine-tuning their sound early in their career. Sometimes no one really wants to know what it takes to succeed. There are also many people whose fish stories are about emotions. They never truly say what they feel or they hide their emotions behind the action. Perhaps they never learned to be vulnerable or are afraid emotion might overwhelm them.

Sometimes people tell fish stories to those they care about because they don't think they want to hear the truth, or they feel the truth might hurt. They pad the facts, leave out the details or fudge the edges sometimes with the best of intentions. It is a matter of discernment to know what story to tell in any given moment.

> Stories are selective. What you leave out is as important as what you include in a story, and sometimes more so.

This doesn't mean you can't make your stories good stories, but it pays to have a more critical eye on where you've adapted them to make yourself look good or for expediency's sake, when honesty is a better bet.

Where have you been telling fish stories when you really need to be telling the truth?

Take action...

Have a critical look. When or where have you been telling fish stories? Why? What are you hoping to achieve? Perhaps there is a NO FISHING sign up in some part of your life, a place you never share stories about. Why there? What's the difference between this part of your life and the rest of it?

Where do you need to tell the true story? Is there somewhere you need to tell the truth? Why would that be a good thing to do? What does that story sound like? How would you need to prepare yourself?

Where is truth asking to be told? Perhaps there's a story in you longing to come to the surface. Maybe there's a story you want to tell, but it has a load of emotion attached to it. How could you let this story out? Do some journaling about this theme and see what arises.

 **Have a look...**

Be an observer over the coming week. Where are you noticing fish stories being told around you? (Why? What impact does this have?) Who around you is very truthful — however you define that — in their storytelling? What can you learn from them?

WEEK 19

What story will unleash what is waiting inside you?

 **Think about...**

There is a Greek word that sums up this idea of "oak-treeness." It is the word *entelechy*.

It is a blueprint of the full being inside any living thing. From the kitten that becomes a cat to the tiny seed holding the potential of a sequoia tree — one of the largest living beings on the planet — everything that has life has potential. Can you get a sense of that potential of YOU inside you? How can you give it voice? Where can you encourage it in others?

So much of what we might be is already inside us.

When you are born, your body already has the potential to be the height it will become when you are an adult. At the moment of birth, you already have intelligence and the gifts you might express. You also have the potential for all types of diseases, errors in judgement and failings.

Each of these good and bad possibilities are merely potentialities. They depend on the nourishment you receive as a child, what training you got about your place in the world — including race, gender, social standing, ethnicity, and beliefs. What you experience, how you grow, whether you get the love and encouragement you need are also important elements.

So much in your life depends on what gets triggered, both positively and negatively, what meaning you make of it, and what stories you carry that influence your view of the world and your agency in it. That's what makes the story of siblings so fascinating. They grow up with the same parents and under the same roof, and yet the trajectory of their lives may be dramatically different.

Agency is your ability to take action. Agency doesn't depend purely on the circumstances you have been dealt in life. It also depends on whether you can see and live into your potential.

There is a famous Hassidic story in which Rabbi Zusya recounts a dream in which he was taken to heaven and comes back trembling. When his followers ask why, he answers reluctantly. They eventually find out he is not asked to be a famous hero or a world-renowned leader. He is not asked to be a savior or a saint. He is not asked to be someone else at all. No, he is asked to be fully and completely *himself*. And being very wise, Rabbi Zusya knows this is a very tall order.

Just because you are no longer a child, it doesn't mean that the possibility of your potential is gone. Seeds have been found in Egyptian tombs that are over a thousand years old. They still sprouted once they were planted in good soil. You can find and awaken your potential even now. It is waiting for you.

If you were to grow into a tree, what kind of tree would you be?
Let yourself drift into your imagination. See yourself walking down a sunlit path surrounded by many trees until you come to a clearing. In that clearing is a wonderful tree. See? Over there, with the sun shining on it. What kind of tree is it?

Have a closer look in your imagination at this tree.
What state is it in? Since a tree is also a full ecosystem, it may be in many states at once. Look it over carefully. Perhaps one part is healthy and vibrant and one part is dying.

One part might be fruiting and the other has bare branches. What does the bark look like? Perhaps there are some lumps and bumps from old woundings or weather damage. Take careful note. Describe the state of your tree as fully as you can.

- What environment is the tree standing in, now that you take a closer look?
- What creatures are living in or with this tree? What is their relationship to the tree?
- What does this say to you about the story of your life right now? What do you need to pay attention to?
- Imagine yourself able to see beneath the soil to the tree's root system. What does it look like? How wide and deep does it stretch? Is there enough of a root system to support the canopy? What is the state of the soil? What is it made of? How is this tree being nourished?

Tell a story about this tree's future. If this tree would be vibrant, healthy, flourishing in the future and leave a legacy for the environment around it, how would the story unfold? What is its relationship to the surrounding ecosystem?

Mandy Harvey's[22] dream almost died. She knew herself to be a singer, but then she became deaf. Have a look at her performance on America's Got Talent and see how she determined to go after it anyway. She decided she had enough of a root system to flourish again.

> Just because you are no longer a child, it doesn't mean your potential is gone. You can find and awaken it even now.

WEEK 20

Who do you want to be and how can your story help you get there?

Think about...

A friend once told me that his Aikido master always said each moment of each day was simply practice for the next moment.

He said that gave him spaciousness. He was able to experiment with new things and risk failure instead of trying and failing to get everything to be perfect. *What can you do now that will help you practice the YOU you most want to be?*

Boiled down to its essence, this teacher's message is that what you are in this moment is simply the result of the choices you've made up to now.

Some of those choices were simple, like *I'll wear the blue shirt* or *let's have the chocolate cake*. Some were more random, like turning right or left, deciding to talk to the person standing next to you or choosing to take the bus instead of driving. These choices have consequences, but you can't predict what they will be. Take the bus ride, for example. You might be late for work or you might meet the person of your dreams. Who can tell?

The choices we make are founded on the stories we tell ourselves. By shaping our choices, these stories determine how far we can go.

Other choices have more profound impacts on you and others around you. How you demonstrate your leadership, or how you exercise your power. How you treat people in relationship, or how you handle conflict or disappointment, all shape your life in extensive ways.

The choices we make may seem to be unrelated, but they are all founded on the stories we tell ourselves, the stories of how the world works and how much agency we have to change it. By shaping our choices, these stories determine how far we can go.

So often our stories are unconscious, shaping our decisions without our awareness or consent. When we become triggered in life, we can be sure that an experience has pinged up against a storyline we are carrying. Becoming conscious of your own stories and how they are at work in your life is the first step in taking charge of the person you want to become.

Take action...

Reflect again ... In Week 5 you were asked to write a fairytale about your life. At the crossroads you received instructions to leave something behind. What was it? As you look back now, so many weeks later, what do you now see about what you were asked to leave behind?

You were also instructed to pick something up and take it with you. What was that? How has this been traveling with you and what do you now understand about it?

What impact will both of these actions — leaving something behind and picking up something — make in your life from this point?

Who do you want to be now? In this day and age, it may seem strange to think that there was once a politician who cared enough about his personal attributes to try and change them for the better. Benjamin Franklin did. Perhaps that is why he became an internationally recognized statesman, well respected by all, a prolific inventor and thinker, someone who had a hand in creating the foundation for what would become the United States of America. His autobiography is well worth reading.

In it, he talks about choosing the personal attributes he wants to foster and on focusing on them with diligence. What are the attributes you want to foster? How will you focus on them? (And a hint here, Franklin focused on only one for a certain amount of time and then moved to the next, and so on.)

Create an epitaph or a eulogy. Pretend you are observing the ceremony around your death and you have been exactly the person you dream to be. What will people say at the ceremony? What will be written on your tombstone? What would need to change in your personal story for this to become true?

The Last Word **is a 2017 movie about a controlling businesswoman who also wants to take control of her legacy.** She decides to contact the local paper and make sure the obituary writer is properly instructed on her job. After a rocky start, the two begin a friendship with life-changing consequences. In deciding to determine how her story is told, the story changes.

WEEK 21
What story can help you experience what you dream of?

 *Think about...*

The beauty of stories is that we can try them on like a new jacket or a different pair of shoes.

Through magnetic imaging and brain scans, which show activity in the form of light, scientists have discovered that when we're engaged in someone's story, our brains are lighting up in exactly the same way as the storyteller's. We are experiencing the story together at the same moment. *What new reality or dream do you want to try on?*

There are many places in the world right now where it isn't very safe to try something new. Of course, trying something new is the root of innovation and discovery. You can't experiment if there is no place to do it, yet if you keep doing what you've always done, of course you'll get the same results. What a conundrum.

Many of us get up in the morning, dress ourselves in a costume for work, instead of what we'd rather be wearing. Or we write an upbeat post on social media instead of sharing how we're really feeling. To the question: "How are you?" we always answer "Fine!"

We want to look courageous, happy and well-adjusted when, inside, we might be screaming. We might be so sad or afraid we don't think we can go on. Or we feel overwhelmed by just trying to keep it together. Maybe we're so tired we just want to pull the covers over our heads. Or we might be bored.

We dream of a life of adventure, of chucking it all in, getting rid of everything and taking a backpack on the road. We long to leave the responsibility and the grind behind us. We talk about leaving the "rat race," about "finding ourselves" or searching for our passion. Maybe, just for a moment, we want to *be* someone else, *doing* something else, *somewhere else*.

The amazing thing is that *in a story, you can!* You can go to exotic locations, get involved in adventures and experiences, feel what it is like to be petrified taking a risk or bolder than you ever thought possible. You can try on another age, stage, gender or background. You can come up against great challenges, wonder if you'll ever make it and overcome them all. And you can do it all inside your imagination.

Stories are like the flight simulator for a pilot — they allow you to have all the engagement and none of the risk. They allow you to practice and experiment in the safety of your own mind. They enable you to be curious, innovative and free enough to dare.

Perhaps imagination is the greatest gift ever given to a human being. Let's exercise it more!

Take action...

What do you dream of? If you could do something, anything, right now, what would it be? What would you do as your livelihood? What would be your areas of expertise? Where would you travel? What relationships would you have? Make a list. And dream BIG.

What would you do differently in everyday life if you had a script and the talent of a great actor? How would you handle that challenging meeting coming up or the in-laws you feel so annoyed by?

Maybe there's a person or group you've always wanted to connect with, but don't know how to start. Write these down too.

Create your stories. Begin by making the most of your senses. If you have a meeting coming up, visualize the room you will be in, down to the smallest detail. What does it look like? Feel like? What is the lighting, the decor? If you dream of traveling, what does your dream location sound like? Smell like? Feel like? What would you see if you turned around?

Now add the other characters in your story, and the storyline. What happens? How does the action unfold? Who are you being within this story? **Try it on for size.** Really *be* in this story.

What have you learned? Just because it is a story doesn't mean that you won't feel anything or learn anything. If you take this on as virtual reality (without the headset) you'll come closer to what stories can do. They are a way of trying something out without ever leaving home.

Have a look...

It is an old movie now, and not a very well known one, but *The Thirteenth Floor* (1999) plays with virtual reality on a whole new level. It is the story of an organization which has created a virtual reality game where players can jump into the bodies of people at an earlier time in order to have different experiences. When someone is murdered and a detective goes to investigate, he discovers the game is larger than anyone dreamed. A more recent take on story as virtual reality is the 2018 movie *Ready Player One*[23].

> Stories are like the flight simulator for a pilot — they allow you to practice and experiment in the safety of your own mind.

What you should actually be trying to figure out is how to tell your story. The one that is every bit as unique to you as your fingerprints. This is the truly amazing feat because you are literally the only person capable of doing that. *Only you know all the parts to your story* and only you can pass it on for others to hear if you choose to.

ASHLY LORENZANA

WEEK 22
Which of your stories is waiting to be told?

 *Think about...*

Inside of you there is a compelling story waiting to be told.

You are the only one who can tell it, but perhaps you are afraid to begin. What is it about? Where does it lead? Why would anyone want to listen? Don't worry about that — *just begin!*

I often talk about *"big S"* stories and *"little s"* stories.

Big S stories are those filled with drama, heroism, amazing sacrifice and challenge. I remember being in Oklahoma City for a storytelling conference. There were a number of people invited to tell stories who had been in the Federal Building when the bombing happened in 1995.

One woman's story was riveting. "It was a beautiful day," she began. "I've learned from so many others who have survived disasters that their stories also often begin with *'it was a beautiful day.'*" And then she went on to tell about being in a meeting, standing at the whiteboard with her back to the room when the explosion happened. She turned around to find everyone gone and a gigantic hole in the center of the room. We were there with her in shock, horror and surprise.

This is a *big S* story — a story of an extraordinary happening where life and death are center front in focus. Not many people have stories like that. But they **do** have *little s* stories — stories about everyday challenges, heartaches and issues. Stories about moments when they had to make choices and moments that determined who they would be in their lives.

These stories can serve as doorways and bridges for the rest of us. In fact, **your *little s* story might just save someone's life.** It might show someone they are not alone. It might give someone the key they need to help a part of their life function, or to get back on track, or to be bold enough to do what they need to do. *But only if you tell it.*

We trade stories all the time. It is an act of trust and connection to do so. The good news is that YOU are the expert on your own life. In fact, no one sees life exactly like you do. Discovering and working with your own stories of defining moments is personally rewarding. It could be collectively beneficial too.

Now is a good time to take a look at the stories in your life, choose some and begin crafting.

> Inside of you there is a compelling story waiting to be told. You are the only one who can tell it.

Take action...

If someone asked you to tell a story of *you*, what would you share? For both relationship building and leadership, it is important to be able to tell an "origin" story. A story, or stories, about what makes you, YOU.

This kind of story helps people to understand what makes you tick, how you see the world, where you put your focus and why, and what matters to you. It helps them both to understand your fundamental nature and how to be in relationship with you, whether that is on a personal or professional level.

Sharing this kind of story builds trust because sharing personal history is an intimate act. You reveal something when you share a story like this. And when you do, others feel more free to share.

So what would you say? Think back through your life and choose up to three moments you feel made you who you are today.

Shape each moment you've chosen into a story.

Step fully into the moment you want to work with:
- When and where did this moment happen?
- Who was there? What was their role in the moment?
- What happened, and what happened next?
- What are the most important elements of the moment? Remember, detail is needed, but too much detail smothers the story.
- Why was this a defining moment for you?
- What message do you want to share with your story? This point is the red thread through the story and a way to organize it.

Once you have these, you can begin to put the bones of the story in place. Try your story out on a trusted friend or colleague. If you can, tell it out loud, otherwise in written form. You might want to ask them to give feedback in a form like this:
- *The strongest image for me was …*
- *I'm confused about …*
- *If it were my story, I'd …*

This kind of feedback will help you know if you were successful in getting your point across and whether the flow of the story is smooth or confusing. Continue to shape your story and practice it. Now you have another story to add to your repertoire.

 Have a look...

Have a look at the TED talk of your choice. See if you can identify how the speaker has built storytelling into their presentation. What caught your attention? How did the story draw you into their topic? Why is this presentation so effective? All of this is good learning about how to craft your own story.

WEEK 23

What is your story of everyday courage?

 **Think about...**

What higher purpose or higher power do you serve that is bigger than you are?

Being a hero isn't only about acts of great courage or stamina. Sometimes it can be heroic to say "no" or speak up for someone else. These are acts of everyday courage. *Where can you be an "everyday hero" this week?*

Let's muse together for a moment on what it takes to be a hero.
There are people who make extreme sacrifices in the face of danger to save others. They jump into swollen rivers to rescue a drowning person or bring animals to safety after a natural disaster. That's certainly heroic.

There are people who put themselves at risk to protect something that's special to them. They go into burning buildings to look for a missing child. They stand in front of others being threatened with violence. They speak up about others abusing power or privilege. They stand up for what they think is right even when no one else is. These actions are also heroic.

And then there is what I would call "everyday courage." This is a far bigger playing field. In order to rise to the challenges of the moment, especially those defining moments we talked about last week, you need to practice regularly on the small stuff.

Like being kind when you don't feel like it. Or continuing to support your children even when they drive you crazy. Or making a gift to someone else when you could be feeling resentful instead. Or creating beauty when it seems like no one else cares. Or sticking with the dream of your heart, even when it seems hopeless, by doing one small thing to demonstrate you are still committed. Each one of these small steps gives you more "courage muscle."

Since you are a human, you are a storyteller. Congratulations! You didn't have to earn this. It is inherent within you. That also means that you are living inside your own story and, therefore, you are the *hero* of that story.

You're the only one who can decide how the hero responds to his or her fate. You are the only one who knows the hidden inner resources the hero will call on in the moment of need. **You are the one who can take charge of your story because YOU are the only one who can decide for yourself what it means.**

This is YOUR story. *What kind of hero will you be?*

Take some time to dream. In Week 16 you thought about your life as a story with you as the central character. What kind of story did you think you were living in? What kind of central character are you? Now reframe yourself into the hero. Make a little drawing or doodle of yourself and surround this little you with the attributes you dream of for your hero persona.

Now make a second ring and think about the actions that demonstrate these attributes. If you wrote "strong," then what actions or behaviors would indicate this strength? If you wrote "compassionate," then what does that look like?

There are so many ways for any attribute to be expressed. What is *your* way?

What does the hero do now? Think about the situations you find yourself in right now — at home, at work, in your leisure time. What are the challenges you are facing? If you really stepped up as the hero in your story, what would you do now?

Write down your scenarios, followed by "and then...." Write how the story evolves when the hero comes on the scene.

Take some time to really observe this week. See if you can catch other people being the hero in their own stories. What attributes are they demonstrating? Why do you think that is? If they aren't playing the hero, then what role are they playing and why? What about you? What role are you playing this week? How could you support yourself and others to step up to hero status?

> Practice regularly on small acts of everyday courage. Each one of these small steps gives you more "courage muscle."

Myth is like a forcefield charging the incidents of our personal history with meaning and significance. It sustains and shapes our emotional attitudes, it provides us with life purposes, it energizes our everyday acts, it gives life meaning and momentum, and it leads us into our *Higher Destiny*

JEAN HOUSTON

WEEK 24

What can you learn through taking a mythic view of your life?

 *Think about...*

The moment you use a simile such as "life is like a journey" you are engaging in the mythic field.

Whatever journey that is — the one that starts in Middle Earth and takes the one ring back to where it was forged, or the one where the rebels plan to blow up the space station — doesn't matter. Being on the journey begins to color your experiences and your actions. *If you look at your life from a mythic perspective, what changes?*

These days we often use "myth" in the same way we use the word "story," in a derogatory sense. We say "that's just a myth!" (meaning it's not true or it doesn't exist) or "don't tell stories" (meaning "don't lie to me"). Some even say the time for myth is over.

In fact, myths will not only outlast all of us, they will probably never go away, because they operate from inside the human psyche. The reason any myth is still meaningful is that it holds an element of truth that is still relevant. Our personal universes, and our national identities, are also bound up with myth.

The mythic field, as Jean Houston points out, helps to give meaning and significance to life. As humans, we are meaning-making creatures. We need to make sense of what happens to us, and stories are the way we do that. Our stories help us to sift through a life that seems to go on like a river, never stopping for a moment. A story is a snapshot in time that enables us to gain an overview and to make meaning.

Even in our modern age, we still get swept up in the fight between good and evil. We follow the course of heroes and their companions with anxiety — *will they make it?* We sorrow when someone or something is lost along the way. We still know exactly what is coming when we see those words *"a long time ago in a galaxy far, far away...."*

We need myths because we need meaning and significance in the ongoing unfolding of everyday life. In the overwhelming minutiae of what it is to be human, a myth is both like a beacon and an opportunity to get a helicopter view of the road you are on.

Take action...

What is your favorite myth? Did you love the Greek heroes or the Norse gods? Perhaps you are a fan of origin tales like the Hopi story of how the world began or how Ranginui and Papatuanuku's children separated them and brought light into the world, as the Maori of New Zealand tell? Find a myth you like and choose it as a companion for this week. What do you notice if you use it as a lens?

HANDY HINT: *If you have a library nearby, you might want to look on the 398.2 shelf, which is where you find myths and legends. If you have a digital book provider, you know what to do!*

Asking for counsel: In the Greek story *The Odyssey*, Odysseus entrusts his household and the upbringing of his son Telemachus to his old friend Mentor. Many times during the story, the goddess Athena assumes Mentor's shape in

> In the overwhelm of what it is to be human, myth is both a beacon and an opportunity to get a helicopter view of the road you are on.

order to counsel the young man, who goes in search of his father and finally welcomes him home. No wonder we still use this term today for someone giving wise counsel!

Now choose a character out of a myth or legend or from your favorite story and pretend for a moment they are your counsel. You might even want to put a chair opposite you and imagine them there.

Ask your mentor about:
- Your strengths and weaknesses
- Where you are in your life and what you need to pay attention to
- Your life purpose or higher destiny
- Advice on what steps you should take next and why
- Their view of the personal story you are carrying

Make notes and see what else comes from your mentor when you do. What have you learned?

Observe the world this week through a mythic lens of the story you've chosen. How does this change the meaning or significance of what you experience? What difference does it make to your energy and momentum?

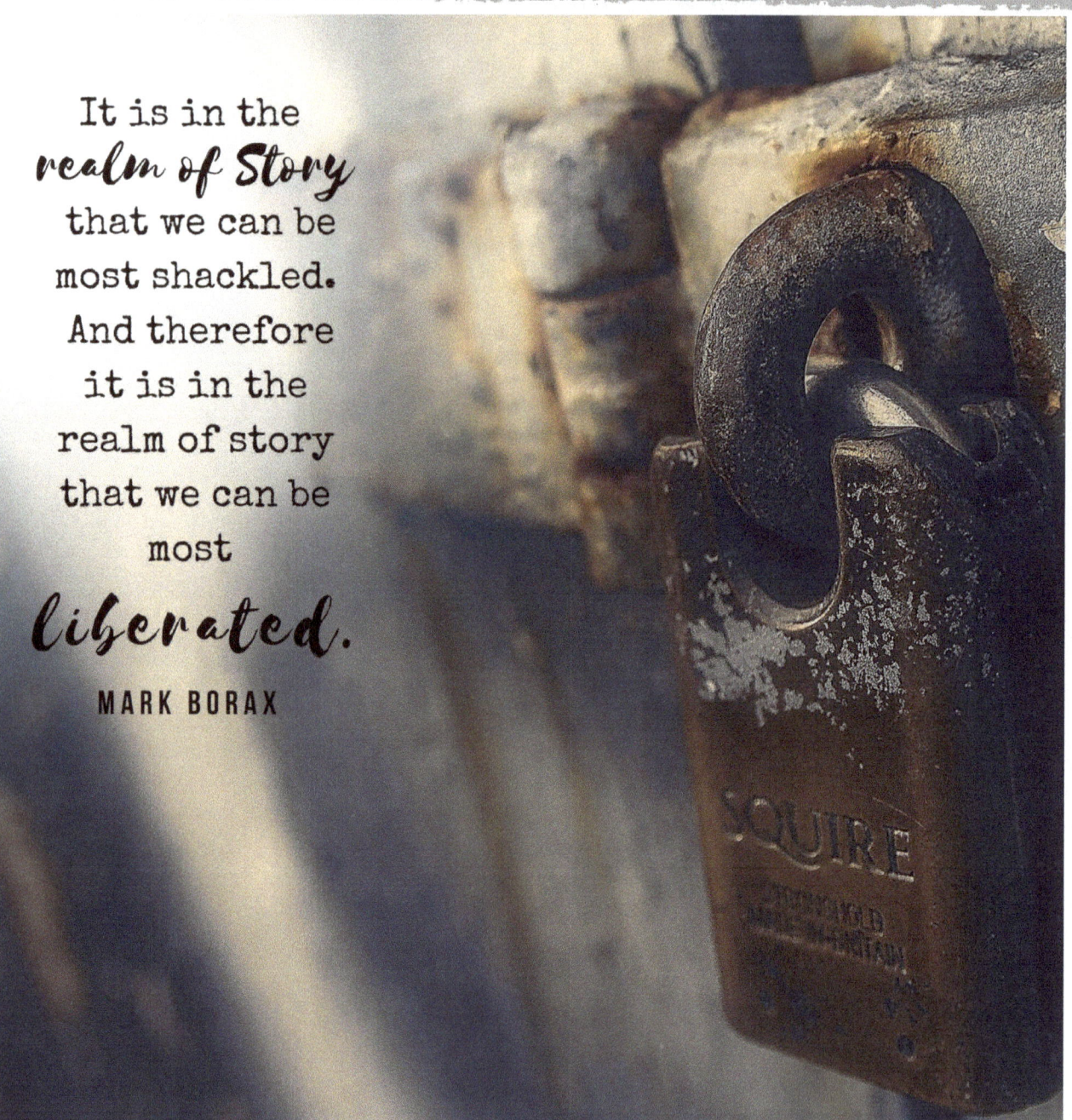

> It is in the *realm of Story* that we can be most shackled. And therefore it is in the realm of story that we can be most *liberated.*
>
> — MARK BORAX

WEEK 25

What stuck story needs to change?

 *Think about...*

Sometimes, the only difference between a closed door and an open window is your story.

It is easy to get so close to something that you can't really see it anymore. What would happen if you stepped back and took a second look? *What part of your story is waiting for a change?*

Sometimes reality can feel like a cage where the door is locked and there is no key. But look again. Is the door really locked, or does it only seem that way? That's the marvelous thing about humans — we are so adaptable. We may not like the situation we are in, but very quickly we adapt to it. Anyone who has moved to a new house knows this well. Often they say: *"I must change that (fill in the blank) immediately!"* and five years later, it is still in the same state!

The body shows us this continuously. It is constructed in such a way that it will make larger and smaller adjustments in order to keep our eyes level so we can make our way in the world. The longer the back or neck are out of alignment, the more the body adjusts. Eventually, this contortion becomes the "new normal."

We treat our stories the same. If the story we find ourselves in is painful, we try to adjust, even to the point of defending ourselves against seeing it any

> **A story is a mutable thing. It can shift, it can offer new gifts, it can change. And in doing so, you change too.**

other way. *"That's just the way it is,"* we say. Or *"I'm fine, really."* Or *"I could never make a change like that!"* Or *"I love them; I'm sure they will change!"*

Sometimes our stories seem so precious or so defining of who we are — even if that is a victim — that we ignore or avoid any information that might change them. When you try to hold on too tightly, a story can calcify, locking you into a single shape. The story — and you with it — gets stuck.

I remember being with my mother on a day trip. She was driving and telling me a story of loss I'd heard in many forms over the years. I took a deep breath and said: "Can you also see that loss also made you stronger and more empathetic? It has made you the deeply caring person the kids you work with so respect today." There was an icy silence and I thought for a moment that she might stop the car and put me out by the side of the road. But later in the day I heard her speaking about how her life had given her strength.

A story is a mutable thing. It can shift, it can offer new gifts every time you look at it more deeply, it can change. *And in doing so, you change too.*

Take action...

Where is there still a stuck story — a story that's more a closed door than an open window? Over the past weeks you've been looking at the facets of your own story and in Week 12 you identified a stuck story. Where is there still a story that feels like a closed door? Where are you telling yourself *"I can't until"* or *"not yet"* or *"I don't have any power"* or *"I'm not enough"*? Make a list of these stories or places in your life.

Take a look back and gather the gifts. Two weeks ago, you imagined yourself as the hero. Last week, you got some advice from a powerful friend. Putting yourself in the hero's shoes, armed with some good advice, what would you do with your story or stories now?

What are the possibilities? Look at the gifts you've gathered and brainstorm a list of what could happen now.

Take one step. Have a look at what you've learned working with your story or stories and decide on one small step you can make towards change.

 *Have a look...*

Sometimes a story can be so stuck that only someone outside it can make a change. During the *Lord of the Rings: The Fellowship of the Ring*[24], Frodo breaks the deadlock during the Council of Elrond. As an outsider to all the power plays and cultural relationships, he is able to step forward and offer a different view. Who could help you get an outside perspective or break the deadlock?

WEEK 26
What question could change your life?

 **Think about...**

It is a challenging thing to find yourself in the not-knowing.

And even more challenging to stay there. Most of us long for safety and security, so when we happen into that place where we don't know and we can't see what's next, it can be unsettling, or even downright terrifying. We feel like a runner in the starting blocks, ready to burst away at any moment, but unsure of the goal. *Stay there. Keep breathing. Wait.* What happens when the not-knowing continues? This is one of the most fertile moments. If you can allow it.

We've tapped into the not-knowing in Week 13. Then we had a look at confusion, which can be how it begins, and looked for a way to befriend it, to let it in, even see that it came with a gift. Now comes an opportunity to look at it once more and sink more deeply into it.

There's a reason to learn how to deal with the not-knowing — at some point or another, it will return. It is just one of the natural cycles of life. Just as a tree goes dormant in the winter time, what actually happens is that life sinks down into the ground and focuses around the roots. It is a time of rest and underground renewal. This cycle in nature reminds us that we, too, need a time of stillness and refocusing.

Where is that place in your story and your life where the not-knowing is showing up? Where are things falling away? Where is the place of *breakdown*? This is also the fertile ground for *breakthrough*.

Sometimes, in working with your own storyline, you uncover stories you don't like or places where you've kept yourself stuck. Perhaps you've been holding onto these stories because they form a large or crucial part of how you see yourself. Self-definition is a vital part of identity. When you begin to drop these stories, there is a void, while your internal map reshuffles itself. Or perhaps you are longing to change an old story and find yourself bound by habit. Or you've discovered a new piece and are working with your resistance to integrating it.

Western culture trains us to try to take action. To *do something*. I'm encouraging you to **be still**. Let the not-knowing sink into you. **Don't try to find an answer; ask a question instead. What question right now could change your life?**

I was sitting with a colleague once who was very sure he needed to leave his work. But the position was a good one and he was afraid. He told me he had the sense he could look over and see his fear standing there in the corner, watching him. I asked him to consider that maybe fear was here to partner him into something new. I also asked him to think carefully about the verb we would choose. We crafted a question for him that sounded like this: *How can my fear partner me in dancing into my next contribution to life?* He still didn't like working with fear, but he was willing to try. Within five months he left the job, learned mindfulness in the Himalayas and was hired back to teach it.

Learning to work with questions builds your story muscles! A powerful question — the one that makes you tremble — can act as a magnet to a new story. A question is like an open door, inviting in new perspectives. And a question, like a story, is irresistible to the neural network. Your brain literally cannot resist it. If you find a question that is powerful for you, your mind will keep working on it, whether you are aware of it or not.

Just like a potent story, a question will cause new ideas, new connections and new possibilities to bubble to the surface. The next part of the journey begins.

 **Take action...**

What is this journey you're on really about? Beyond your desire to be seen and recognized, beyond your striving for wealth or power or position (whether that is as a CEO or an entrepreneur or as the best in your yoga class) what is your lifelong journey really about? What relationship do you have to life purpose? What question could help you explore this?

Consider questions like: *What matters most to me?* Or *If I could do anything in the world right now, what would it be?* Or *If I knew I had a short time to live, what contribution would I still want to make?* Use these as a starting point.

Formulate a question in your own words and let it sit with you this week. Put it on a sticky note on your bathroom mirror or on a sign on your desk. Keep reflecting and seeing what arises. You might want to keep asking yourself: "So what then?" or "What's beneath that?" Don't give up too soon! More and more gets magnetized as you keep on working with a powerful question.

What is your real work? There is work and then there is *vocation*. A vocation is something you are uniquely capable of doing, something that makes your heart sing. It is that contribution you feel you are here on Earth to bring. You might be a manager, whose true vocation is bringing out the amazing potential of those around you. Or a parent who is gifted in creating an environment where children find their gifts and know how to exercise them. Or perhaps you are a natural gardener and this is simply what you do anywhere you are. This is the work your heart is called to, regardless of whether anyone else knows about it. Can you name this work?

If you are living your vocation, congratulations! What is the next iteration or unfolding of it? If you are not, what would life be like if you did?

> Learning to work with questions builds your story muscles! A powerful question can act as a magnet to a new story.

What story are you carrying about your work? Take time to have a look at the stories you are carrying about work. What is "valuable" work for you? What does success mean? Where does your work, your passion and the needs of the world intersect? What needs to change about your work story to enable you to take the next part of the journey?

How do you know if your life's work is really done? In this blog post, former chairman of BCG India, Arun Maira[25] focuses on this question and on a line from the Bhagavad Gita: "You only have a right to the work, and not to the fruits thereof."

What questions could change my life?

Choose the one that makes you tremble!
Share your questions with the *365 ALIVE!* Community.

WEEK 27
How can slowing down help you see more?

 **Think about...**

Our world is moving at an ever-faster pace.

Far from helping us become more skilled at grasping the nuance of things, this pace means we can miss out on the small signals that indicate an opportunity is on the horizon. We can get so mesmerized by what's flashing by that we fail to see what is right in front of us. What will help you slow down and notice what's in front of you this week?

The human brain has evolved over time to keep us safe. Over eons of dealing with wild animals and threats of all kinds, our fight-or-flight mechanisms are hardwired into our way of approaching the world. This helps us scan the immediate vicinity for dangers, but it also means that our brains operate on a "first fit" pattern recognition system, rather than a "best fit" system. If it is big and yellow and roaring, who cares if it is a lion, a leopard, a cheetah or something else? *RUN! RUN NOW!!!*

Our story pattern recognition system is similar. We compare every story we hear with every other story we've ever heard. Our brains are constantly scanning for patterns. So when someone says: *"Have you heard the one about …"* we are poised and ready. **Bingo!** *It's one of those.* We've categorized it as fast, or even faster, than we can listen to the words.

Most often, we categorize things into the patterns we are already holding. It is as if each of our stories are puzzle pieces, which fit together to form our own unique map of reality. We navigate the world by this map. When a new puzzle piece comes flying in our direction, it locks into place with others already there, it can be easy to extend our map of the world. But when the piece is very different, something that doesn't easily fit, we can either disregard it or defend ourselves from it. That means we can be blind to a new potential.

I remember visiting Montezuma's Well in Arizona. It is an artesian well of bubbling fresh water and has been a meeting point on the trade routes of the Americas for centuries. Shells came from the Pacific Ocean, bright bird feathers from South America, pipestone from Minnesota, and they all met here.

It was early in the day, so no one else was there. I moved slowly, avoiding the places where signs said rattlesnakes like to bask in the sun. Finally I sat next to the water, with a tangle of brambles beside me, and drank in the scene. It took some time for me to notice my companion — a tiny green frog on one of the branches.

Some time later, a group of friends came walking along talking loudly to each other. I wonder what they took in from the place. I wonder if they noticed me. I can be quite sure they never saw the frog.

Opportunities can be like that frog, hiding in plain sight. But if you never slow down, if you don't stop to be observant, you may never see them. Perhaps your next big opportunity is right where you are, hiding in plain sight.

> It is as if each of our stories are puzzle pieces, forming our own unique map of reality. We navigate the world by this map.

Take action...

Decide to slow down the pace this week. It seems the larger the place we live in, the faster we walk and talk. People get used to bustling about, wolfing down their food, rushing to the next appointment. This week, change your mode. Focus on the word *spaciousness* this week and decide to become part of the SLOW movement. Take time away from your desk. Savor your food. Walk more reflectively without the intent to get anywhere. Look slowly and appreciatively around you. Take time to listen before you jump into conversation or action. Decide to be HERE, right where you are, and focus on the now. Rest in the moment. *What happens as a result?*

Learn the difference between *hard* and *soft* focus. Most of us use a penetrating gaze on life. We want to know what is happening and what it means. This "hard" focus is good for taking action. But if you want to know the deeper nature of things, you need to use soft focus. Look at people and things gently, encouragingly, with a desire to be open to them and with the intent to truly know them. This soft focus encourages things to come to *you*, rather than you chasing them.

There are things only YOU can see. As you know from all our work up to now, you have a unique lens on the world. There are things that only you can see because of your unique perspective. So take that spaciousness you've been practicing and turn it on the world of opportunities. Perhaps you love music. What music can you hear underneath the surface of the day-to-day you haven't recognized before? Perhaps you love your animals. If you looked at the world in the way they might perceive it, what would you see?

If you really listen to the stories people are telling, if you really stop to feel how you are resonating with what life is offering you, if you SLOW DOWN, what opportunities can you catch a glimpse of? How does this change the story of your journey in life?

One of the most beloved stories on the planet is *The Little Prince*[26], Antoine de Saint-Exupéry's 1943 classic tale of an aviator who is forced to land in the Sahara and there meets a strange young man. The book has been translated into 300 languages and still sells around 2 million copies a year. In one scene, the little prince meets a fox who schools him in what it will take for them to create a relationship. The word used in the English translation is often the verb "to tame," but French speakers will tell you the word the author used has more the sense of "befriend." Either way, to befriend someone takes time, patience and persistence. And still, it is one of life's most worthwhile endeavors. Have a look at what needs befriending in your life.

WEEK 28
What seeds do you want to water now?

 **Think about...**

Perhaps you've heard the story of the two wolves, the one about a grandfather helping his grandchild to see that there are two wolves inside every human heart.

The bad one and the good one. These wolves are constantly fighting, each one trying to defeat the other. "Which one will win?" asks the grandchild. "The one that grows is the one that gets fed," the wise grandfather tells the child. It is the same with our stories. The ones that keep getting told are the ones that will keep growing, and the ones that will be our lens on the world.

This is the final stage in Part 2 of *365 ALIVE!* and a time to review how far you've come. Over the past 23 weeks — almost half our time together! — we've been focusing on you and your story.

We began by asking you to climb the mountain and have a look. To do this, you wrote your own fairytale as a beginning to this inward journey. You met and befriended your inner critic. You looked back into childhood and combed through your memories. You took the helicopter view and stood in the messy middle.

You considered where your stories might be stuck and how to help them breathe. You had a look at pain and embraced the not-knowing. You looked at what story you find yourself in now, reflected on yourself as the hero and considered your own honesty.

Then you took a look at your own potential and how you might try it on for size through the power of story. We looked at life as a mythic construct and considered what doors and windows might lead you to the next big opportunity.

Each of these pieces is like a fractal of the greater you. All of the angles we've looked at were like polishing the facets of a diamond — together, they make it possible for the light to reach the heart of the gemstone and dazzle the eye. Remember, a diamond is merely a piece of coal that withstood the pressure of time and was polished by a skilled hand.

And here we are. It has been quite a journey, and a story worth telling! *Great work, fellow storyteller!*

Reflect back … Take a look at the work you've done up to now in Part 2. We've approached it week by week; now take a look at the whole. What do you see? What stands out? Ask yourself:

- What have I noticed about my own personal field of stories? Who influenced it? How was it shaped?
- What can I see about the arc of my story over my lifetime? How has it changed? What are the consistent themes?
- Which stories or storylines are holding me back right now? What do I want to change?
- Are there any areas of my life I've avoided? Are there stories I'd like to spend more time with?
- Which stories or storylines are lifting me up right now? What do I want to strengthen?

- What are the most important things I've learned about myself on this journey so far?
- What are the most important things I've learned about story and storytelling so far?

Which seeds do you want to water? StoryWork is the work of the patient gardener. Much has to be done before the flowers bloom or the fruit is ready to pick. A gardener envisions the future and then begins to create it. First the ground is prepared. This is the work we have been doing together. Then the seeds are planted, watered and tended. This is the work you do through diligent practice. Finally, the fruits are ready to share, and your stories begin to travel in the world.

But more importantly, you are the person who is prepared to listen, who notices what needs to be told or who needs attention. The work on story is work on yourself, honing you to be a contribution in the world.

So look back now with the eyes of a gardener. Which stories will you stop tending so they can wither and die away? Which stories will you water so they can bear fruit? What story practice do you want to foster?

Have a look...

In the US, scientist Bill Nye is known as "Bill Nye, the science guy." He makes his living making science understandable to ordinary people and often uses humor to do it. In one of his blog posts[27], Nye reflects on how science and comedy have been two compelling threads in his life story.

> Which stories will you water so they can bear fruit? What story practice do you want to foster?

PART THREE

Story at Work in the World

In the work I've done hosting groups over the past twenty-five years, I've noticed that listening is both an intensely compassionate act *and* a greatly needed one. It is a profound demonstration of our attention and care.

We have developed a modern culture that is predicated on making the most of time. We rush to get out of the house in the morning, we work to pressing deadlines, we take pride in overworking or being available at all hours. We manage to sandwich in meetings with friends, but our devices are constantly at our sides, drawing attention. Even our speech has become quicker and more punctuated.

This elevates the sound bite to an art form, within an ever-increasing pressure to be heard. We feel harried and overwhelmed. We seem to always function with a time deficit.

The important thing to realize is that stories have a certain pace to them. Listening is best done slowly and with intention. We need to clear the decks and step out of our own mind chatter. Those who study listening remind us that it happens not only through the ears, but through our combined senses, our experience and our attention. It is a whole-body activity.

But even more than this, I've realized that listening is vital to collective health and well-being. All of us need to feel deeply and respectfully listened to, no matter our differences, before we can listen to others. This is more and more apparent in the global breakdown of public discourse as we fall into more black-and-white thinking and become more polarized around issues.

In **Part 2** we worked with our own stories, paying attention to our own inner worlds, in order to create the ground we need for listening to others. This is vital foundational work. If you want to be helpful in the world, you need to become intimately connected to your own story material and work with it so you are aware and in charge of the stories you are carrying. Otherwise, when you get triggered, the stories may run away with you, leaving you less room for curiosity, compassion and creativity. When you know your own stories, you know and can trust yourself. This enables you to listen to others more fully. It makes you more response-able in any situation.

In **Part 3** we will turn our attention outwards, looking at how stories work in the world and asking you to take the role of a **Story Activist** — someone who activates the positive power of story for and with others. In the coming weeks you will learn about others, and even more about yourself. In this process every look outward has the power to be another step inward on your story journey.

What are my learning goals?

Share your goals with the *365 ALIVE!* Community. Look for inspiration.

WEEK 29
Stories help us make meaning

 **Think about...**

Human beings are all about meaning.

In fact, most of us don't do very well if we feel we've lost the meaning of our lives. We feel adrift or marooned. Some of us find meaning in a sense of achievement or contribution. We find it easier to give than receive. Some of us need to see a higher purpose in life. Some of us need tangible goals or people to cheer us on. Somewhere each of us has absorbed or created the story we carry about what matters to us and what it takes for us to matter. *What is the source of your sense of meaning?*

Often we are so wrapped up in our own lives and times that we can scarcely think about the rest of the world. We are busy handling our home and work responsibilities and we feel as if we don't have time to put one more thing on the action list. But come with me and zoom out for a moment. Let's take a look at humanity.

No matter where a person is born, grows up or lives, we all have something in common. **We want to belong** and **we want to matter.** We want to belong to our family, our "tribe" and our community. We want to be intrinsic to the weave of that community. We want to feel and know our place, to be *home* in the deepest sense of the word.

We also want to be recognized as respected individuals, to have worth and value. We want our voices to be heard and taken into account. We want to make choices and express ourselves. We want to know it mattered that we were alive and we were here to family, to friends and to the wider circle of humanity.

In the Western world, we want to be respected for our uniqueness and value. In more socialized cultures, we want to know we have fulfilled the dream of our ancestors, taken care of our community obligations and lived a well-regarded life.

Our sense of meaning and mattering is tied up with our well-being. Our sense of belonging is an important measure of mental and physical health. When we can't find connection and we can't see we matter, the thread of the story of our lives gets knotted beyond recognition or broken altogether. We feel abandoned, lost and meaningless. Is it any wonder that some people suffer from severe anxiety, have mental challenges, turn to violence or even try suicide?

No matter where a person is born, grows up or lives, we all have something in common. We want to belong and we want to matter.

We are at a critical point in our humanity's broader story where it is easy to feel as if the old story is broken and the new one not yet here. Old power structures are trembling while many of us try hard to shore them up. Disasters and despots have unleashed a flood of humanity onto the highways and byways of the world, shaking the stability we thought was here to stay. What had sense and meaning yesterday might have none today.

Being aware and awake can be very helpful in times like these. *How can you work with story to create sense and meaning for yourself and others?*

Where can story help us create more meaning in life?

First, think about your own sense of identity. Turn inward for a moment and focus on what matters to you and where you draw your meaning. Explore your beliefs with these prompts:

- *"I am a ..."* There are many roles you play. What are they?
- *My skills are ...* There are many talents you have and ways you can be useful in this world. What are they?

- ***People turn to me for ...*** What do others recognize in you or seek from you?
- ***What really matters to me is ...*** What is it? What are you passionate about or have energy for?
- ***And if all of that were gone ...*** What is it at your core that is your essence? What shows up when you show up, no matter what?

What is the story of YOU now?

Become a StoryCatcher[28]**.** During the coming week, find the opportunities to listen to stories of others. You might ask them:

- What is it like to be *you*[29]?
- What matters most to you? What is it you are most passionate or committed to? Why?
- Take me to a moment in your life when you felt you'd made a real contribution. What was it?
- When people talk about you, what do they most comment on? How do you feel about that? Is there something you hope they'd notice?
- Was there a moment when you really felt seen by someone? What happened?

Take the time to really listen. In doing so, you are reinforcing the value and worth of the person you're listening to. That, in and of itself, is a great gift. But you are also exercising your muscles as a StoryCatcher and this will help you be both a better listener and a better storyteller.

What have you learned through listening?

We're not all alike. Sometimes, that can be challenging. But what if we could include all the differences and act as if we all had meaning? What would that look like? Try it out, with the short video *Inclusion Starts With I*[30].

> The best *Stories* are like the best burgers: big, juicy, and messy.
>
> —A.D. Posey

WEEK 30
Stories make sense

 **Think about...**

Some things are better messy …

… like huge hamburgers or overloaded pizza when you're hungry, or volcanic mud pools when you want to do something great for your skin, or fingerpaints if you want to totally express yourself. Why should life be any different?

It's kind of strange when you think about it, but so many things in life are messy. Anything having to do with children or relationships is a good place to start. As Shakespeare so aptly wrote: "The course of true love never did run smooth." But this messiness extends throughout much of life.

Both getting into, and out of, life — more commonly known as birth and death — are messy affairs. So are creativity and innovation, no matter how much we portray them as a straight line afterwards. Living together and being in community sounds like it should be wonderful, but sometimes the opposite is true.

What about confusion or communication breakdown? *Messy.* What about interactions between people? *Messy.* What about trying to learn a new skill? *Messy.* What about moving to a new job or a new place? *Messy.* What about trying to sort out the difference between what you want and what you need? *Messy.* What about the inside of your own head or heart? *Messy.* (Am I right?)

In fact, you could almost say that anything having to do with a human being is probably ... *messy*.

That's why we love stories. We are living in this ongoing, barely controllable mess that keeps lurching towards tomorrow, but through a story, we get to take a look at a slice of life. We can make sense of that much. We can try it on for size, and feel satisfied that there's a beginning, a middle and an end. We can take a bite without having to gulp down the whole thing. ***Stories are human-sized.***

One of the most important things stories do for us is help us make sense of the mess we live in and the mess we make.

What messiness can story help us make sense of?

Try out your listening. Help someone else make sense this week. Look for an opportunity to ask for, and listen to, someone else's story this week. It might come naturally as part of a conversation you're in, or you may need to make an invitation. Here's a guide:

Make an invitation: "I've been thinking about how stories can help us make sense of things. Is there a part of life or work you're trying to make sense of right now? I'd love to hear about it."

Be an active listener: Pay attention to the storyteller with respect and interest. See if you can remain present throughout the whole story. This can be challenging, because your mind will want to bring up stories or comments of your own. Don't interrupt. Let the other person have space to share. If they get stuck, that's the time to ask a question.

"What sense are you making of this situation right now?" Ask for the storyteller's view of what's going on. Listen closely. Remember, you build trust and relationship when you listen (and you always appear wiser).

Thank them for their story. Be sensitive to whether the other person wants input or not. You might want to test this by asking them.

Take a moment to review what you've heard and see if there's a gift you can find in the story for the teller. The biggest gift you can give someone is *yourself* — paying attention to them and receiving their story. The next biggest is to help them see more facets of their story. This doesn't mean solving their problem for them, but helping them to see something for themselves. What new or other perspective can you give from what you've heard?

What have you learned as a result? Listening is a compassionate act, but it is also a skill and an art form. If you want to be a better storyteller, you first need to be a better listener. Then you will truly know that stories are everywhere.

If you want to learn more about listening, take a look at Chapter Two in the book *Momo*, by Michael Ende. He spends the entire chapter describing the listening ability of his main character. She's my role model for transformational listening!

What else did you learn?

Have a look...

How do you make sense of music, if you're deaf? A group of American Sign Language practitioners are changing the deaf experience of music. See how they are doing it, in a short video called *How sign language innovators are bringing music to the deaf*[31].

> You could say that anything having to do with a human being is probably ... messy. That's why we love stories.

> If you remember the pleasure of hearing a story many times, you will remember that while you were listening you become three people. There is an incredible fusion: you become the storyteller, the protagonist, and you remember yourself listening to the *Story.*
>
> MARINA WARNER, "FROM THE BEAST TO THE BLONDE: ON FAIRY TALES AND THEIR TELLERS"

WEEK 31

Stories give us connection

 *Think about...*

Stories are so embedded in our human psyche that they operate on many different levels simultaneously.

When we hear a good story we are immediately in it, moving along with the characters. We begin to care about them and that piques our interest. As we talked about in Week 21, because story calls on imagination, our brains light up in exactly the same way as the storyteller, so we stand in their shoes. We feel what the teller is feeling, as if we are inside the story. At the same time we are the listener, receiving the story and being stimulated by it, so our own stories rise.

There's another thing that happens when stories are being shared — our brains automatically release oxytocin, the feel-good neurochemical that is connected with a sense of safety and community. This chemical enhances empathy and our ability to experience others' emotions. The chemicals and neurotransmitters our brains release, and the way they light up around stories, are different than the way we receive data or information. We become connected to what we hear in stories in such a way that we can carry all they hold with us, sometimes for a lifetime.

> Stories are the mycelium sheath for humanity. Once we've shared stories, we can never see the other person in the same light again.

There is plenty going on at the same time, so it's fortunate we are wired for stories. Scientists say that we may even be coded for story before birth. No wonder it comes naturally.

I have a slightly different way to talk about this phenomenon. For me, it is as if we sink down and grow a root system together. In the same way that the mycelium sheath — the mushroom kingdom — is the connector and nourisher of trees and the wider ecology, so are stories the connectors and nourishers of human culture. Once we've shared stories, we can never see the other person in the same light again and there is a foundation to move forward in a new way. If the connection is strong, common ground can move to higher ground.

Much of this has to do with the power of witnessing. As humans, we need the sense we have been seen and recognized. To witness something fully is deeper than listening. You might say the word *witness* could also be called "with-ness": the ability to share someone's reality, if even for a moment. Stories invite us in by giving us a window into someone else's experience.

What connections could story help us make?

When have you felt connection? Think back and find a moment when you felt very connected to someone else after hearing their story. Ask yourself:
- What was it about their story that touched me?
- How did I feel when I heard their story?
- What did the story provoke in me?
- What did my response make me want to do?
- How did I demonstrate my connection?
- Why does this moment stay with me?

Where do you want to foster connection? Where in your work or life would you like to have deeper or stronger connections? Think about how you could create the space for some storytelling. **And don't worry, you don't even have to call it that!** Just ask a question that opens the way for a story, like: *"I've been thinking a lot about trust recently. When was a moment you experienced trust within a team?"* or *"I'd really like our next trip together to be fun for everyone. What trips have you heard about from other families that sounded fun?"*

You may have to go first to open the way, but if you do, more stories will follow. One story usually sparks another — think about how it is amongst a group of friends out for dinner. If someone tells a story, others will contribute with their own.

If someone consistently offers an opinion, say: "Have you got an experience to share?"

Mohamed Bzeek[32] is a man with a big heart. He knows how it feels to be facing fear alone and that made him open his home to more than 80 young people abandoned by their families. The short video *Man's home is a haven for dying kids* is his story of fostering sick children.

WEEK 32
Stories are a frame for imaginative possibility

 *Think about...*

The beauty of stories is that we can get inside them and see them in our mind's eye.

Because of imagination, the places in the story have the colors we give them and the people are dressed as we choose to see them. The objects are as we imagine. Things take up the space we decide. Our imaginations are at play. *Is it any wonder that we don't all agree or see things the same way?*

Involving the senses is an important part of good storytelling. We can do this by using language that helps people imagine something the way we want them to see it. If we don't do that, they will make it up anyway. That's just how the mind works. Our brains are set up to try to make sense of everything, so they automatically fill in the blanks. It is good to be aware of this natural human tendency.

Sometimes when I'm working with a group, I like to demonstrate this fact. I tell them a little story about me on my bicycle rolling along the streets of Copenhagen. I go on and on with this made-up story until I suddenly turn to them and ask: *"What color is my bike?"* You'd be amazed at the variety of answers!

Stories help us make sense of something: Hey! What just happened? And they also help us make meaning: What does that mean to me now?

Sense and meaning are two different things. Stories fulfill both of these functions. They help us make sense of something: *Hey! What just happened?* And they also help us make meaning: *What does that mean to me now?*

I saw a very powerful demonstration of this some years ago in a training session I was hosting. We had asked the group to work in trios and to share stories of courage. One of the participants told a story of moving his family from New Zealand to the US to take up a new job. A week later he was asked to take up a dangerous assignment in another part of the world and he agreed. The team ended up getting kidnapped! He told this story as an example of his own courage.

But his team had another idea. They reminded him he'd forgotten another key player and the courage she also demonstrated. The family had moved in the winter time and landed in their new home, in a new country, in the midst of a snowstorm. He'd left on assignment a week later and she had to hold it all together until he was freed.

With tears in his eyes he told the group: "That happened twelve years ago, but tonight I have to go home and tell my wife what I've learned."

Through a different set of eyes, and through the power of listening, this story took on a new facet and a new level of depth. The storyteller's group helped him to find new meaning within an old experience and a new perception to the concept of "courage."

How can a new perspective change the story we're living in?

 Take action...

Choose someone you trust to share a personal story with. It is a very common thing for people to share an important personal story with a meaning already set in their mind. This is especially true when it is a "working story," meaning you are telling this story to gain support or funding or market share. Or when it is a family or community story that is told again and again.

It is easy for such stories to become polished in a certain way. But then they also become one-dimensional. Having a new pair of ears on your story is one way to freshen your perspective on it.

- **Invite a friend or trusted colleague to support you** by listening to the story and making meaning.
- **Decide together what you'd like them to listen for.** Perhaps a new set of eyes can help redefine who you were in this story. Perhaps you'd like them to listen from the perspective of another player. Or maybe you'd like the helicopter view of what you can learn from this situation. Giving your listener a lens with which to view the story helps them to focus.
- **Tell your story,** not artfully and smoothly, but with heart and intention — with authenticity. Allow the story to touch you again.
- Turn to your listener and **ask them to share** what they've heard through the lens they were listening for.
- **Share your responses** to what they've heard. What did you learn from what they said about your story?

Practice supportive sense making. When you are with others, practice listening with a purpose. Decide to listen deeply and attentively enough that you can contribute to the person you're listening to. If you find a new perspective, ask first if they are open to hearing it. Decide to be a **Story Activist,** someone who activates stories for a more flourishing future. If the teller is not open to a new perspective, in what ways does their story make you personally curious? What new perspective can you find for yourself?

What makes a good life? A Harvard study[33] on happiness is one of the world's longest running, following its subjects from youth to old age to try and assess what makes a good life.

WEEK 33
Stories help us honor and integrate our woundings

 *Think about...*

Emotional resilience is needed to listen to challenging stories.

This kind of resilience means you have the courage to stay present, to stay with someone else's story, rather than falling into your own. This quality of compassionate witnessing is so needed in the world. But first you need to be able to be with yourself. *What practice supports your ability to stay present with yourself and others?*

When was the first time you realized you weren't perfect or you didn't fit in? Some of us got wounded at home when we weren't seen or recognized for our unique qualities. Or we learned at school that we were different from the larger group of people around us. We had a different language, accent or different customs, a different faith or family construction, a different skin color. Maybe it was when we were old enough to be out in the world and were excluded because of our different preferences or ways of expressing ourselves, the way we acted or our different way of seeing the world. Or we felt awkward and out of touch, as if we would never fit in.

Some of us turned off our creativity when we were told we couldn't draw or sing or play an instrument to the standard others could. Some of us noticed that our physical prowess was lacking or we didn't look the same as others — we were bigger or smaller, lighter or darker, we didn't look like the popular crowd or we were more differently abled in some way.

Some of us look quite normal on the outside, but carry our wounds on the inside. We were hurt by people we trusted or we felt abandoned or betrayed. Power was used against us and so we use power against others, or against ourselves. Hurt people, hurt people.

One of the first steps in dealing with scars is to be able to witness them. To take them as a badge of surviving whatever it was. To say, "It's okay not to be okay." Acceptance first, and deep witnessing, not fixing. Then, when it is invited, helping ourselves and others to find the potential strength that comes out of the wound.

This is one of the most beautiful ways we can serve others and they can serve us. It takes strength — strength of heart, strength of mind and strength of character. It is very challenging to give up a wound because so often identity is built on it and the sense of meaning we take from it. In response, build your emotional resilience by focusing on what keeps you balanced.

What are the practices you regularly undertake to stay present? Do you run, swim, meditate, do yoga, exercise, play with your kids, get enough sleep, nurture relationships, garden, make things, talk to friends, read, write, sing, dance, volunteer, interact with your pets? What helps you stay in balance? Deepen your practice so you can stand the strong stories that need to be heard so wounds can heal.

What supports the emotional resilience to stay with challenging stories?

Reflect on your practice. So many people say they have no time to cram another thing into their lives, but is that really true? Ask yourself:

- **What do I do to numb myself?** Do I get lost in social media? Spend hours on Facebook? Watch too much TV? How addicted am I to things that take me away from being present?
- **How often do I take time to sit quietly without having to DO something?** How often do I do nothing and allow myself to be? How comfortable am I with silence?
- **How do I honor my emotions?** How often can I just be with them, rather than trying to fix them or make them stop? How comfortable am I with strong emotion?
- **When was the last time I really observed my surroundings with curiosity?** How easy is it for me to just observe and take things as they are, rather than making judgements about what I'm seeing?
- **What are the practices that help me to be present, to really show up?** What happens when I really take in the world? How easy is it for me to stay present, especially when I'm around something/someone that triggers me?
- **When was the last time I felt deeply listened to?** What happened inside me then? When was the last time I deeply listened to someone else?
- **What is the most important thing in my life, the thing that really brings heart and meaning to my life?** What attention is it receiving? Is that the attention I'd like to be paying to it?
- **How do the stories I'm telling myself support or undermine the practices that help me feel present?** What am I prepared to change so my practice can truly be the foundation of me feeling that I have agency in my life?

What are the woundings you're carrying? Take some quiet, personal time to reflect.

- **Think back to your childhood.** What are the woundings you gathered from this period of your life? How are they still playing themselves out now?

> Helping each other to find the potential strength that comes out of wounded stories is one of the most beautiful ways we can serve.

- **Consider your teenage years and your young adulthood.** Which woundings came from this time? Which are still with you now?
- **Think about the rest of your life.** What woundings have happened since? What is present and active now?
- **Consider your dreams and hopes.** What hurt or woundings are you carrying from dreams that haven't manifested or hopes that were dashed? What can you do to honor and release this hurt?

Spend the coming week listening in on the stories you are telling. How are your stories reinforcing or exacerbating your woundings? What victim roles have you talked yourself into? Which stories are offering you a doorway to a new perspective or a new way of perceiving yourself? If there are not enough of these, what stories do you need to begin telling?

It is a powerful story when two people decide to pursue healing. The TED talk *Our story of rape and reconciliation*[34] is a powerful story because both of the protagonists decide to commit to staying with the healing and confronting the original incident.

What needs to be honored?

What action(s) will help you integrate?

WEEK 34
Stories help us take back our power

 **Think about...**

Not long ago I was listening to a powerful story of what it has been like to live in Greece during a time of financial crisis and systemic breakdown.

We heard about what the Greek people had been learning as things fell apart. They were forced to return to what they have long known about coping with very little. It was also a story *about* power and how you begin to find yours again if you feel it has been lost.

One thing the storyteller said really struck me: "We've learned that if you don't return to your fundament, the ground practices of your ancestors and their ancient connections to the land, you become fundamentalistic."[35] Those who have no ground, or feel their ground cut away, or are threatened, can retreat into fear, creating stories and actions that help them feel in control or return to "the old days." The challenge is, these stories and actions are often used to try and control others.

We see this tendency throughout history as structures that have been in place for a long time begin to break down and the old stories no longer serve. It is difficult and often painful to be in confusion or contradiction. In striving for the perceived certainty of the old order, we can become polarized and more black and white in our thinking.

In times of uncertainty, it feels easier to put feelings of unease outside of ourselves, blaming bigger forces or others for our challenges, imbalances and troubles. We can force others to hold the shadow for us, demonizing whoever we define as "the other." This is the time when stories can be used as weapons. We are in a time when dramatic rebalancing is needed.

The ancient Greeks knew a thing or two about stories. They say that for anything to happen, there must be a mixture of three great forces. First comes **Gaia**, or Earth. There must be grounding for something to happen.

Next, **Chaos**. There needs to be a little chaos for something new to arise. If the same elements are always in place, if stasis happens, then nothing new will be born. Mixing new things together makes change.

Finally, **Eros** or erotic love. Without a passionate spark, how could new life come into being? Without fire, nothing gets heated up, nothing expands. Love and passion provide the opening. When these three forces come together — *kapow!*

What a different pattern this offers than striving for control! Find your ground, lean into chaos, bring love with you — or invite it in. Paradoxically, you may now have more power than before.

Take some time this week to track the flow of stories around you. Who has power over their own story and who doesn't? Where can you let go a little control over someone else's story? Where do you need to take back the power of your own story? What happens as a result?

How will you support others to take back the power of their story?

Become the witness again this week. Step into the role of the witness (remember the stance of "with-ness") and continue to hone your powers of observation.

> Instead of controlling, find your ground, lean into chaos, bring love. Paradoxically, you may now have more power than before.

- Who does or does not have power over their story? Where do you notice people being "storied" by others? What about groups in your organization or community? Your children? Others in the world? The moment you hear *"All (fill in the blank) …"* or feel the assumption of this, you are hearing a group being storied by someone else.
- How often do you try to "story" others? What assumptions are you holding about others and their stories? What do you do (or not do!) to find out what their stories really are?
- Where do you feel someone is trying to "story" you? When do you notice that others are trying to tell you what your story is or what it means? What happens as a result?
- Where are assumptions alive inside of the stories around you? There are assumptions inside of the stories you're hearing. Can you find them?
- What is the dominant narrative? Can you listen for the dominant story inside your organization? Your community? Your nation? Your family? What is it? Is it a generative one, or if not, what kind of quality does the story carry? Who are the leaders in this story? Who are the heroes? How do others show up and why?

What will you do to take back the power of your story and support others to take back theirs? What can you do to become more awake and aware of the stories active around you? What choices can you make about the stories you pay attention to or the ones you feed? What story are you living in now and which do you want to be living in? What is the first step towards activating this new story?

What do you do when you are not like others but you want to live your own story? A short video called *Nineteen Paper Cranes*[36] is a slice of life from Japan.

Think about the word *destroy*. Do you know what it is? **De-story**. *Destroy*. **Destory**. You see. And *restore*. That's **re-story**. Do you know that only two things have been proven to help survivors of the Holocaust? Massage is one. Telling their story is another. Being touched and touching.

Telling your story is touching. It sets you free.

FRANCESCA LIA BLOCK
"BABY BE-BOP"

WEEK 35
Stories help us reclaim ourselves

 Think about...

We touch each other with our stories.

Sometimes stories are healing, opening the doors of the small spaces we inhabit when our thoughts run around in circles or make a mess. And sometimes stories become a prison, confining us below ground, in the cellar of the mind. We feel stuck there, pounding on the door, asking for release, but no one hears or brings the key. In this case, a story can become like a dead weight, pinning us down and feeling almost impossible to shift.

Sometimes we do that to ourselves, but often, we do that to each other. Often this occurs through restricting someone, or a group of someones, to a single story.

Every human, every thing and every place is multi-storied. Every person is a walking StoryField, an intersection of all the stories they are holding about themselves, all the stories others hold about them and all the stories they are part of through family, culture, race, ethnicity, gender, place, connection and experience. You might say we are walking libraries, even though some of us have chosen a specific section, shelf or even genre to focus on.

Every generalization, every stereotype, removes the complexity of a person's StoryField, reducing them to a single story. This de-storying makes it easy to make judgements, to classify people, label them and to treat them differently. Although this happens quite naturally in the mind as a way to organize and make sense of the world, it is a habit we need to be aware of and guard carefully against. Generalizations make our lens on the world simpler, but also more simplistic. In removing the complexity, we also remove the richness and the potential.

In the same way that a place is bulldozed, removing the visible history, a people's history can be bulldozed, buried, denigrated, retold from another's vantage point or obliterated completely.

Where have you or others been de-storied? And where is re-storying needed? Re-storying begins by opening the space to hear others' stories and other stories about people, places and things. What would enable people to touch and be touched so that a reweaving of the StoryField is possible?

Taking time to really listen is a first step in supporting people to reclaim the richness of who they are and to honor the legacy of what they carry.

How can you support others to reclaim their stories and themselves?

 Take action...

Dedicate yourself to listening this week. How much do you really listen? Try some of these:

- **Sit outside with your eyes closed.** Spend at least five minutes in silence, deeply listening. How much can you hear? Give yourself permission to hear *everything*. See if you can do this with great attention, but with little effort. What reveals itself when you listen like this?
- **Decide to be totally present during your next meeting.** Test your listening capacity by seeing how much you can take in during a meeting. See if you can stay present as others speak. Keep your

mind focused on what matters to those speaking. Don't try to plan what you will say, but paraphrase others first before making your contribution. What happens as a result?

- **Choose someone you care about and tell them you'd like to listen to them.** Take it slow. Invite them to share. Listen from the attitude of curiosity and wonder. Feedback to test what you've heard is correct. What happens to your relationship as a result?
- **Deeply listen to yourself.** Give yourself some dedicated time alone. Take a piece of paper and divide it in half lengthwise. Write to yourself and ask questions with your dominant hand. Answer yourself with your non-dominant hand. This may be challenging, but stick with it! What do you learn from yourself?
- **Reflect on what has been de-storied and what needs re-storying in your community, country or the world.** What is calling out to be seen and reclaimed?

Re-storying begins by opening the space to hear others' stories and other stories about people, places and things.

Have a look...

Decide to dedicate a few hours to free listening. Join the Free Listening Movement.[37] Yep, this really is a thing!

WEEK 36
Stories help us remember who we are

 **Think about...**

Stories are meant to be shared.

There's an old Indonesian tale about a young boy and his old servant. Every night the servant tells stories, but the boy never tells them or passes them on. The stories are forced to live in a leather bag behind the door. It is cramped and horrible and they finally decide to take revenge, each in their own way. *Our own stories are like that.* Some stories can fester and begin to poison the one who holds them. What stories in the world right now need to be told so they, and the people who hold them, can change?

Although I love stories and understand that my internal world relies on them to make connection, I didn't grow up in a house where stories were the currency. My relatives (for the most part) were not story people. I didn't have grandmothers who told stories of the old days or aunts and uncles who told stories about being young, or taking risks, or what it meant to be a good man or woman. When I meet people who had this growing up, I sometimes feel envious.

My parents were shaped by the Great Depression. My father took part in World War II and his father in the one before. They were silent men, enigmatic. My parents didn't entertain much at home, so there were few conversations to listen in on. I didn't grow up in the House of Stories; I think I grew up in the House of Secrets. That makes me value stories even more.

From the stories I do know about my family, I've learned that things which might have been scandalous in their day, feel tame or even curious today. Something shifts for everyone when the great burden is laid down and the story is set free.

Throughout all of human history, we've told each other stories to know our place in the world. Stories help us to know why things are the way they are, and how we need to act as members of the local and global community.

But we also know what it is to colonize each other. One of the most powerful ways we do that is to stop others using their own customs, speaking their own language or telling each other their stories. The Native Schools set up in North America and Australia are powerful examples of attempting to destroy and de-story a group of peoples. They were designed to "take the native out of the native" by "civilizing" them and making them useful to the dominant society.

This process was not only incredibly painful to the families, creating "stolen generations," but also devastating to the cultures of aboriginal peoples. It could rightly be called *soul loss* — a categorical losing of place and purpose in the world. It resulted in early mortality, addictions, disease (or more rightly dis-ease), dysfunction and a dearth of meaning, leading to disconnection and lack of agency. This fundamental rip in the storyline is playing itself out today in the extreme rate of youth suicide in Greenland, persecution of Roma people in Europe, healthcare issues in the US, the disappearance of native women in Canada, marginalization of Aboriginals in Australia, child soldiers in Africa, sex trafficking around the world, and so on.

These are not the only casualties. All of us are suffering from the predominant consumer and economic myth that sees us having more stuff, but less time. More online connection, but less real time relationship. More focus on cyber

"Likes" and less on embodied joy. The less we connect with nature, the more our human nature, our wild nature, and our story nature suffer. We have forgotten so much, but hope is not lost. We are storytellers still.

What stories need to be told now to help us remember who we are?

Take action...

What are the stories of your lineage? Take some time to find your own story foundation. What are the stories of your ethnic heritage? Your culture? Your family? Your belief system? How are those stories influencing you today?

Where are there gaps in the storyline? Where are there people who have disappeared or those no one talks about? What are the secrets that are also a part of you?

Where will you decide to take action? What needs to be reclaimed in your own family storyline?

Whose story is not being told or not being listened to? Choose a focus and take some time to research.

- **Who were the original people in the place where you live?** What was their story? What does this story say to you about what you experience now in your place? Look for the deeper stories of people.
- **What did your place look like at that time?** How has the geography changed since the time of those original people? What about nature and animals? What does that say about how people are living on this land now and how they are treating it? Look for the deeper stories of place.
- **What are some of the local customs and rituals?** What is their history? What are we still enacting that has its roots in an older story? Look for the deeper stories of rituals and celebrations.
- **Consider hopes and dreams.** What hurts or woundings are being carried by people or place around you? What dreams manifested or

> We have forgotten so much, but hope is not lost. We are storytellers still.

didn't manifest for people and place? What hurt or woundings are you carrying from dreams that haven't manifested or hopes that were dashed?

- **What communities or groups of people need to tell their stories and be heard now?** What are those stories? How could you be helpful?

Pick any aspect of nature and find myths, legends or tales about it.
Why does the sun go across the sky in the way it does? How did people come to be on the Earth? What is our connection to animals? What were the transition places between this world and another? Pick a topic and research it. What do you feel and understand as a result?

The Australian movie *Rabbit-Proof Fence* is the true story of two aboriginal sisters taken away to boarding school. The older sister takes the younger and begins the long walk home, and she does it twice. This is not only a brilliant movie, but a well-researched one, which includes a learning guide and advice for teachers as part of the DVD.

A note to myself to remember...

> Somewhere, something *incredible* is waiting to be known.
> — CARL SAGAN

WEEK 37
Stories help us share the incredible

 **Think about...**

Carl Sagan[38] spent his life looking up.

He loved the cosmos and the stars and he taught millions of others to love them too. His foundations were the seemingly opposite qualities of skepticism and wonder, an ideal combination for a scientist. Today, declare yourself ready to know the incredible. Keep stillness within you to hear the quiet invitation.

With all the shouting in our media and all the things clamoring for your attention, it could be easy to forget that the incredible often announces itself in a whisper.

A dragonfly shimmers into your peripheral vision. The bud of a flower opens imperceptibly. A small stream starting in Minnesota grows to become the mighty Mississippi. The plumes of mist rising from the crack in the ground announce themselves as the Zambezi River, the one the locals call "The Smoke that Thunders." The atmosphere shifts gradually around the mountain called Fuji-san so much that the people there talk about "tasting the air." Healing waters pour out of the earth in so many places. And you need to be the height of a plane to get enough of an overview to perceive the wonder of the Nazca Lines in Peru.

There is someone sitting not so far away who has an amazing dream. There is another who has performed an act of courage few can believe. And yet another whose family sacrificed everything so they could be here, right now, for the future generations. Perhaps that 12-year-old over there will find a cure for one of our generation's major diseases. The potential within humanity is unfathomable.

Sometimes, by sitting in nature and letting the mind go, you can just sense the web of life. There is a connection that is tangible; a humming energy that is palpable. A sense that you are a very small part of something much, much greater than you can ever imagine. It is the sense of how tiny you are in the scheme of it all, that same feeling as when you look into the Grand Canyon or you lie beneath the stars in the South Pacific.

There are more mysteries around us and within us than we can ever count. Maybe that's why stories exist. They help us to put words around those things that really have no words. They help us to share our experiences, deepen our reflections, relive that part of the greater mystery we've touched.

But you'll never know, if you don't ask, you don't wonder and you don't look.

How can stories bring back our sense of wonder?

 Take action...

Where is your sense of wonder? When was the last time you used your sense of wonder? Get it out, polish it up, and apply it this week. Your job is to find at least one incredible thing each day this week. Be curious and open to where you might find the incredible. Nature is a good place to start. Ever watched an ant colony or seen a spider weave a web? What about the patterns people make on the streets or patterns clouds make in the sky?

At the end of the week, write or tell the story of your incredible journey. Be sure to share it with at least one other person.

 Have a look...

I love the films of Japan's Studio Ghibli. *Princess Mononoke* is one of my favorites and 2017 marked its 20th anniversary. Directed by Hayao Miyazaki, it tells the story of man's battle with nature. Inflicted with a deadly curse, a young warrior named Ashitaka sets out for the forests of the west in search of the cure that will save his life. What he meets there is an allegory for human life today.

Especially touching is the scene when the Spirit of the Forest touches down on a pool of water. If this were an American film, this moment would have been marked by a glorious fanfare of music to let us know something incredible has just happened. In this movie, the moment is marked by silence.

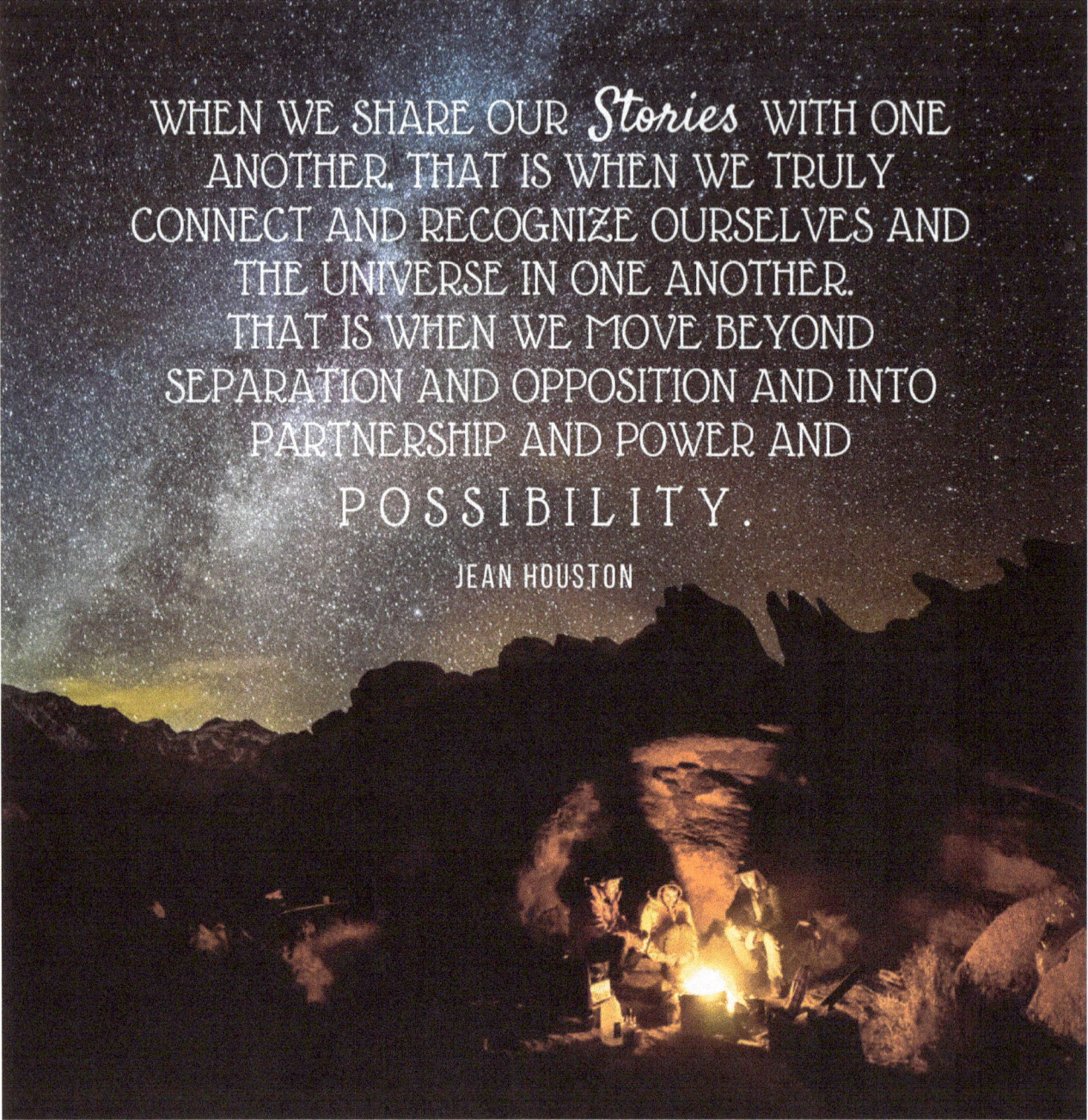

WEEK 38
Stories awaken possibilities

 **Think about...**

There are plenty of disasters happening in the world.

Often, even with the destruction of life, property and livelihood, community arises. People find each other, protect each other, risk their lives, perhaps in order to save the life of someone else. For a time, everyone feels as if they are part of something greater, connected by the same circumstance. *Stories can work like that.*

Stories work in the human mind to connect us. When we resonate strongly with someone's story, the brain releases dopamine, which stimulates the pleasure centers, and oxytocin, which makes us feel safe and gives us a sense of community and belonging. It's a little like falling in love.

When stories hit our emotions, they make us take action. No emotion, no action. Stories give us the possibility to use our power for some purpose; they give us a sense of direction and agency.

Scientists tell us that the brain is capable of holding everything we have ever learned or experienced. During brain surgery, they've proved this by

> **Stories give us the possibility to use our power for some purpose; they give us a sense of direction and agency.**

stimulating different centers and hearing people speak about experiences and memories. The challenge for most of us, though, is finding what we know amidst all that is stored in our brains.

The brain needs context to find content. That's why questions are so important. A good question can open the doorway to a story. Finding a new or different question can lead to uncovering new stories. They were there all along; it's just easier for the brain to go down its habitual tracks. A powerful question jumps the circuitry.

A stimulating question or a prompt in the form of a word, a sentence or someone else's story makes it possible to sift through everything we've stored in memory to find something specific. Imagine a closet stacked high with shoe boxes containing a wide variety of objects. Chances are, even if they are carefully labeled, you may have forgotten exactly what's there. This often happens when long-term couples get together with new people for dinner. One of the pair might say something the other one has never heard before, and when asked later why they never mentioned it, responds truthfully: *"You never asked!"*

Hearing new stories leads to different conversations, out of which new collective sense and meaning can arise. From this sharing of stories and conversation, we can build common ground. Suddenly, it's a shorter distance to higher ground. We get a glimpse of a different future and we're open to a different nature of reality. More is possible.

What new possibilities can our stories awaken?

What question could change the lives of those around you? Observe yourself and your environment closely this week. What kind of questions do people around you ask? What kind do you ask? Do you hear more answers or more questions? Check on your own and others' question literacy.

If they are mostly transactional or questions seeking facts or information *(What does that cost? Who will be there? What's for dinner? When do we meet?)*, see if you can add some transformational questions into the mix *(Why is that so important to you? What are you most hoping for? What do you dream is possible? If you had a magic wand, what would you do now?)*. Ask your question, and listen. Don't seek to fill the silence, just wait. See what happens.

Use questions to explore stories. Take the question exercise further by asking questions that lead to stories. Some examples:

- When have you experienced …?
- When was your first time to …?
- Have you been scared to speak in public? What was that like?
- Who was your first role model for …?
- What stories did you hear about _____ when you were young?
- What has been your favorite …?
- What do you appreciate/love about …?
- What possibility do you see for …? When have you experienced something similar in the past?
- Take me to a moment when …
- Give me an example …

What are ways to awaken new possibilities at work and in community? Check out Adam Kahane's book *Power and Love*. He digs deeply into social justice issues we are grappling with, taking Dr. Martin Luther King Jr.'s quote as a guide. He says the seemingly-contradictory drives behind these approaches — *power*, the desire to achieve one's purpose, and *love*, the urge to unite with others — are actually complementary.

Storytelling has a real function. The process of the storytelling is itself a healing process, partly because you have someone there who is taking the time to tell you a story that has great meaning to them. They're taking the time to do this because your life could use some help, but they don't want to come over and just give advice. They want to give it to you in a form that becomes inseparable from your whole self. That's what stories do. Stories differ from advice in that, once you get them, they become a fabric of your whole soul.

That is why they heal you.

ALICE WALKER

WEEK 39
Stories are healing

 **Think about...**

From my desk on the first floor I can just hear the muted ring of the Japanese temple bell I brought back from my trip there.

Below the sound of traffic, the lawn-mowing services, the cacophony of neighborhood noises, it is there, reminding me of stillness and beauty. But to hear it, I have to listen. I have to pay attention and tune into it.

The more I work with people, the more I observe how groups interact and stories work, the more I know that paying attention — or, better said, *being present* — is one of the best capacities you can build for yourself. Because you never know when the teacher will appear or the healing will be offered.

At its very heart, perhaps the first purpose of a story is to be heard. All humans seek to make sense and meaning of the world. You've heard me say that often. Our stories form the lens through which we understand our experiences and they shape the actions we take. Each of us has stories to share to create connection and community, to help each other. But the only way that works is if someone is listening. Someone needs to be paying attention.

I was in a circle in Japan when someone decided to tell his story of what it meant to grow up always trying to fit in. He'd done it for so long that he'd forgotten he'd rather have been himself. He'd forgotten his true voice and expression. As a young teacher, he was faced with a pupil who also didn't fit in, no matter how hard he'd tried. Now, years later, that young man realized he'd been faced with a mirror of himself. He admitted that he not only hurt the child by trying to force him to conform, but also hurt himself. It was a profound and deeply moving moment of total honesty.

His raw expression of pain at this awareness opened the door for compassion and also healing, for himself and for the others in the circle. The key to this moment of grace was the attention and deep listening going on in the circle at that moment.

It might seem paradoxical, but when voices around you get louder, it's time to get still. When everyone asks for your answer, it might be time to listen instead. When things seem to be pulling in different directions, it's time to focus into the center. When emotions are high, when people feel stressed, when change is upon you, paying attention and listening deeply enables people to relax enough to focus on what matters, to find trust and pull together.

It begins with listening and attention.

How can we make spaces for the healing power of story?

Take action...

Where do you spend your attention? For this week, keep a log. What do you normally pay attention to? What grabs your attention? What steals your attention? How often do you find yourself *down the rabbit hole* on the internet or lost in social media?

Are you paying more attention to your fears and worries, or to your hopes and dreams? Do you pay more attention to yourself or to others? Is what matters most to you at the center of your attention and if not, what is?

What practice will you take up to become more mindful? Some people meditate, some pay attention to their breathing. There are a wide variety of mindfulness practices. Take up a practice this week and see if you can bring more attention and presence to your days. Often this starts by consciously slowing down. What happens as a result?

When have stories been healing for you? Think back over your experiences. When has someone told you a story that brought you healing or listened to you in such a way that healing happened?

What needs attention or healing for you right now? How do you make space for that? Where can you offer attention or healing through sharing your story?

Emily Wong's claymation film *Such is Life*[40] shows without words how we can hurt and heal each other. We bump into each other, we run away, we give and we take. we reveal ourselves and we hide. Sometimes we feel like bigger forces are trying to get in the way. What does this life mean? Ultimately, we need each other.

> Each of us has stories to share to create connection and community, to help each other. But the only way that works is if someone is listening.

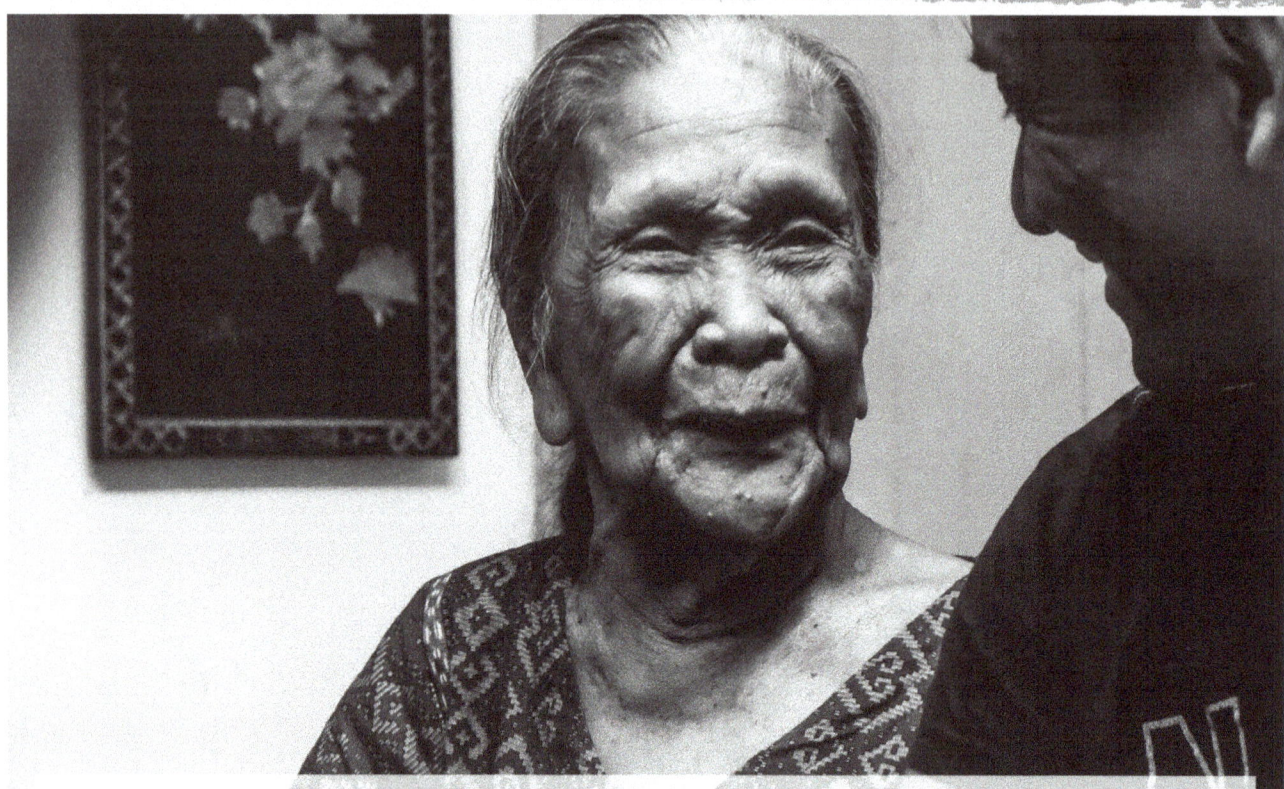

Empathy is the most mysterious transaction that the human soul can have, and it's accessible to all of us, but we have to give ourselves the opportunity to identify, to plunge ourselves in a story where we see the world from the bottom up or through another's eyes or heart.

SUE MONK KIDD

WEEK 40
Stories help us to meet

 **Think about...**

Do you know the difference between apathy, sympathy, antipathy and empathy?

Pretend you are walking down the road and you see a deep hole in front of you. As you approach, you suddenly realize there's someone down there, calling out. You can just see the tips of their fingers waving frantically. *Apathy* means you pay no attention, do nothing and keep on walking. *Sympathy* means you climb down in the hole and cry with them. Now both of you are down there. *Antipathy* means you shout out to them: *"It's your own fault you're down there!"* as you walk by. But *empathy* is a kind friend. You listen, you ask what you can do to be helpful and you do what you can. You stand in their shoes for a moment.

Standing in someone's else's shoes can make all the difference. A colleague once explained the concept of "bubble travel" as the opportunity to leave your own little bubble and travel for a moment in the world of others. It's not as hard as it sounds.

You can bubble travel through movies, or reading books or showing up in places you don't normally frequent. You can talk to people you normally never talk to or serve in a food bank or volunteer. It's helpful to make even small changes, such as taking a different route to work or changing your social routines to be with new people, or eating different foods.

> Through empathy we find a richness in the stories and the world that comes to meet us.

The easiest way, though, is to enter the story of someone else. What can you learn if you look through their eyes? What can you understand if you try to feel what they feel? What would you do differently if you knew someone else's pain or glimpsed their joy? Where do you need to listen to someone else's opinion or experience? How is the world changed when you take a different view?

I was once invited to be on a call with First Nations educators in British Columbia to talk with them about using stories in education. I wondered what I could contribute to a group with such a rich story heritage and culture. I had a plan for some breakout group work, but at that moment the technology failed. I realized that the most important thing I could do for the group at that point was to listen. One of the women shared that her personal story of discrimination at work was dismissed by a colleague. "That never happened!" he said. Of course, I could hear her anger at the incident, but I could also feel the deeper pain of having her experience both denied and erased by someone else. It made me reflect on how power and privilege are used without thinking. It made me wonder how often she has experienced that.

Later, I had my perception of place dramatically altered when I met up with a new friend for the first time. He suggested we meet at a café which he knew I could find easily. We talked for some time and enjoyed the conversation together. Eventually, he remarked that as a black man he had never felt safe on that street. This comment struck me deeply in the heart and I found myself then — and every time since then on this street — looking at it with fresh and troubled eyes.

My experience of the world and someone else's may be diametrically opposed. F. Scott Fitzgerald, the author of *The Great Gatsby*, once said: "The test of a first-rate intelligence is the ability to hold two opposed ideas in mind at the same time and still retain the ability to function." Practicing this is a great way to stretch both your view of the world and your empathy.

If it is true that each of us are facets of a greater whole, how are you enhanced by entering into the world of someone else? Who will you become as a result? Making a practice of bubble travel is a great way to extend your view of the world. As you know, some people maintain that the most common form of travel in the world is between the covers of books. Heading to the nearest library might be a wonderful way to start!

The more we take a look at our blind spots and biases, the more room there is for empathy. Through empathy we find a richness in the stories and the world that comes to meet us.

How can we expand our empathy to meet the worlds of others?

Take action...

What are your blind spots and biases? Which voices do you decide are not worth your time or listen to rarely? Take a look at the books you are reading, the movies you watch and what you pay attention to in the media. What do you notice about your habits? This is an ideal time to change your "diet" and include more diversity. Make a choice to take in more minority voices, to learn about the views of those who have been marginalized or who have a radically different viewpoint. Make yourself a list of new inputs to try. The more you stretch your thinking, the more stories you will be able to hear.

Hone your learning edge. We've worked already on our own story material and discovered some of our trigger points. These pointed out to you where your learning edge is. Take up that edge again now. What other stories do you need to delve into to hone your learning edge and strengthen your empathy? What new experiences could support you in refreshing your view of the world?

Empathy leads to compassion. Remind yourself that feeling empathy does not mean you condone behaviors that are abusive or violent, but you can try to understand and let that understanding foster a sense of how you want to engage in the world.

 *Have a look...*

Dr. Brené Brown is a research professor at the University of Houston Graduate College of Social World and has spent her career studying shame and vulnerability. She has plenty to say about how empathy can work in listening to the pain and suffering of others. Search out one of her many videos on the internet.

What other worlds are waiting for you to discover them?

What makes you curious?

WEEK 41
Stories are way showers

 **Think about...**

There are some experiences that are like signs pointing to the future. You might even call them way showers of destiny.

During my high school days my mother asked me if I'd like to meet Rob. Rob was the son of her colleague. He had just come back from being an exchange student in Japan. He told me what it had been like to experience a culture that was totally different from our own. He explained about a strange and unique food called "sushi" (this was the 1970s, so no one in my hometown had heard of sushi yet). His story was so different to my ears that it awakened a fire inside me. *I was determined to have that experience too!*

I applied to become an exchange student when I was sixteen. They told me I was too young but the fire of the story that burned in me would not go away. I applied again. At seventeen, I spent a year in Germany.

I learned about a new culture, embraced a new language and came to look at the world in a new way. I was no longer only from the place I was born. I now claimed myself as an international citizen. It was a year that fundamentally changed my life. And it came from a story that took root in my heart.

Many other stories have taken up residence within me as well. Some of them are personal stories and some are literary. Michael Ende's book *Momo*[41] has given me a forever role model for listening. Tolkien's trilogy, *The Lord of the Rings*[42], belongs to me personally because I was living in New Zealand during the years it was being filmed and knew people who were involved in its making. Through them, I too was part of a fellowship and an epic journey. I listened to Barry Brailsford tell stories that were part of the *Song of Waitaha*[43], sitting on the stones of the South Island in New Zealand, underneath a blue and windswept sky, and they took up residence in me, too.

The beautiful thing about all of these stories is that I can tap back into them over the course of my life and see what they mean to me now. Each of them helps to illuminate part of my personal journey.

Some stories become beacons. They are maps to new possibilities. They light a fire in us that can illuminate the dark times and give us hope when despair is all around. They can point to purpose, awaken curiosity and give us a sense of meaning.

What way shower stories have you received and shared?

What stories have taken root in you and why? Take some time to search your memory and your foundations. Which stories have taken root in you? Why are they important? What did you learn or integrate from them? They might be family stories, or stories shared by someone you loved and trusted. They might be stories read to you or read by you. How have they shaped your view of the world? How are they still working within you and influencing you today?

What stories are alive and working in the systems you are part of? Which stories are influencing your family? Your community? Your organization? Your networks? What kind of a view are they offering? Are these stories of obstacles or opportunities? How do they impact individuals and/or the collective?

What stories could you share that might make all the difference to someone else's life? What stories from your life and experience (or from the experiences of others) could act as a way shower or a guide in the relationships you are part of? Think through them and make a list that will help jog your memory later on. How will you stay alert to story-sharing opportunities?

 Have a look...

The Harry Potter[44] books are one of the most loved and most influential series of children's books of modern times. In 2018[45] the BBC reported on how themes from the series turned up on signs carried by school-aged protesters in the #NationalSchoolWalkout campaign in the US. Harry Potter themes showed up again during protests in Thailand in 2020[46].

Some stories become beacons. They are maps to new possibilities.

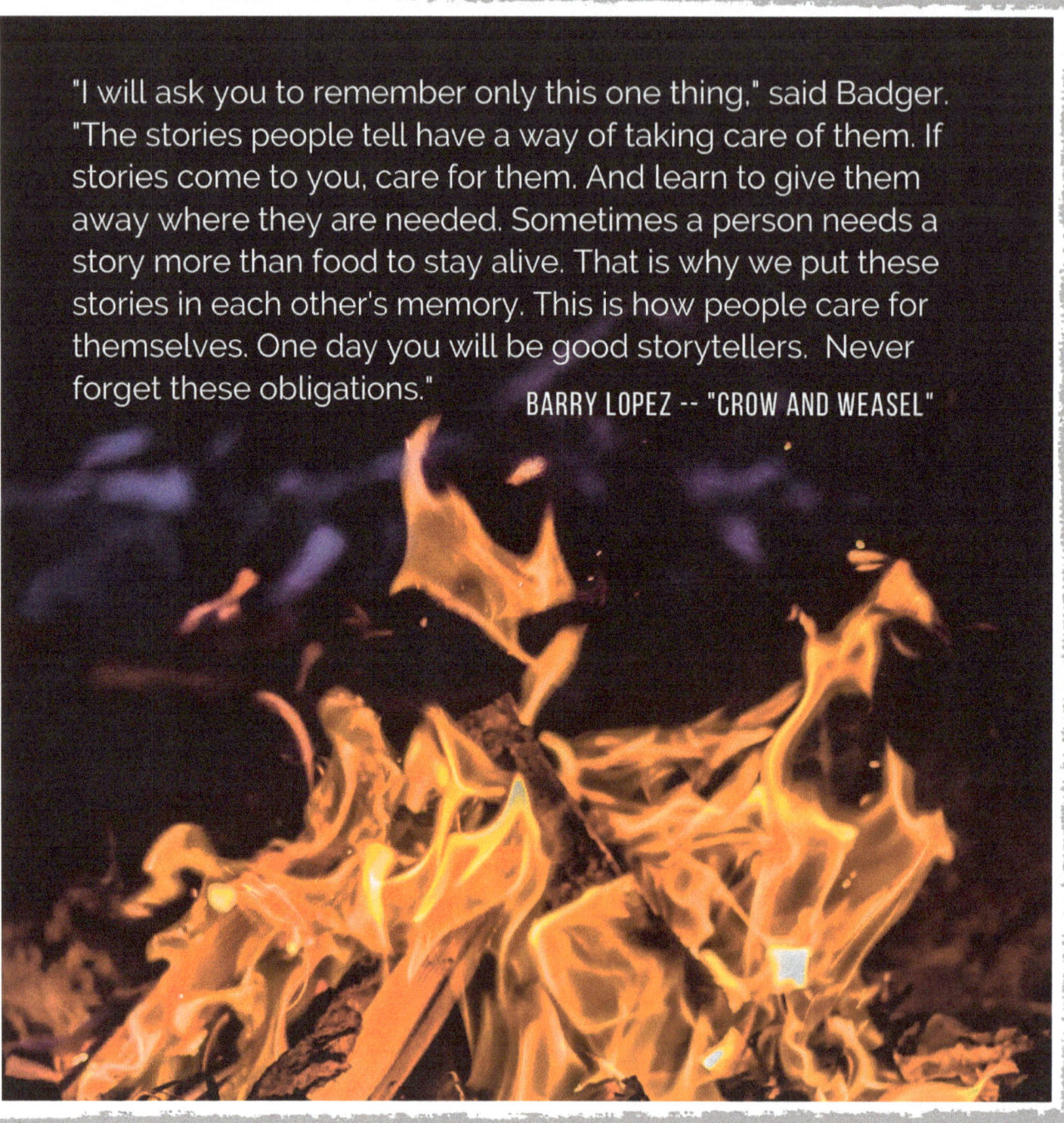

"I will ask you to remember only this one thing," said Badger. "The stories people tell have a way of taking care of them. If stories come to you, care for them. And learn to give them away where they are needed. Sometimes a person needs a story more than food to stay alive. That is why we put these stories in each other's memory. This is how people care for themselves. One day you will be good storytellers. Never forget these obligations."

BARRY LOPEZ -- "CROW AND WEASEL"

WEEK 42

Stories help us care for and hold each other

Think about…

Over the course of my life with stories, I've had to learn how to let them become part of me and speak through me.

I often used to wish I could tell a story perfectly, as a flawless performance. But somewhere along the way I realized that good storytelling didn't depend on words and delivery, but on offering the perfect story for that moment.

At some point traveling in the world, I began to feel I had an invisible basket on my back (the kind women gathering plants used to use) into which I tossed my experiences and the stories people told me. That was the easy part. The harder part was learning to trust that the perfect story would show itself exactly when it was needed and I would be able to tell it. In one of my journeys, a story from Japan served a group in Chicago and its story in turn was shared in Sweden. And so the stories flowed around the globe.

Crow & Weasel[47] is the story of two young people making their way in the world. The advice they receive from their elder, Badger, is important advice for all of us. "If stories come to you," he tells them, "care for them. And learn to give them away where they are needed." Here he calls the two young men to be both good listeners and good stewards of the stories they are given.

Hearing someone's story is becoming part of someone else's life and having their life woven into yours.

Both are valuable life skills, skills they will need in their journey and when they return to their people.

It is often said that sometimes a person needs a story more than food to stay alive. Stories lend us meaning. They are often a light in dark places. They can rally the spirit, they can show a different path. They can pull us up short and make us reconsider reckless action or overwhelming emotions. And they can help us renew the stamina and courage to carry on.

In my work as a facilitator, I often invite participants into sharing stories with each other. While one person shares their story, another one of the trio listens for what can be learned from the lived experience in the story, and the third focuses on what they can learn from the teller. I call this third role the witness. Later I speak to the group about listening as love in action. I ask everyone to treat what they have received as a gift.

Being a good storyteller is both a practice and an obligation. Both care and respect are needed in holding memories in trust. We need to prove to life that we are trustworthy and capable of holding something precious. When we do, stories come our way for safekeeping. This is a loving service we perform for each other, even though we may never know who carries our stories forward.

What stories do you hold in trust?

Whose stories are you carrying? Sometimes we are carrying the stories of our lineage, our family or our community. Sometimes we are holding memories in trust from other times. I feel that way about people I last saw in their twenties who are now more than fifty years old; I'm holding the story of our younger days. Whose stories are you carrying?

What other memories are you holding in trust? Take some time to comb through your memories. What memories remain with you from childhood? What facets of yourself or others do they show you? What blessing can you send your younger self or the younger others?

Realize that once you hear someone's story, you can never see them in the same way again. Hearing someone's story is becoming part of someone else's life and having their life woven into yours. This is a role that demands trustworthiness. How will you demonstrate it? What can you learn from them and their story that might be nourishment for someone else?

How can you grow your sensitivity for story sharing? Knowing *when* to share a story and *which* story to share demands a good connection to your intuition. You need to go with your gut feeling. There are many ways to practice, but here are three: *You wonder what time it is.* Before you reach for the phone or look at the clock, sense it. What time do you think it is? *The phone rings.* Before you look at it, who do you sense is calling? *Someone flashes through your mind and you get the sense you should make contact.* Before thinking, act on this flash of insight — now! See what the response is.

Elizabeth Gilbert[48] is best known for her blockbuster bestseller *Eat, Pray, Love.* However, it is in her book *Committed* that she describes the weaving together of her own story with her soon-to-be-husband's. There is a beautiful scene in the book in which they are lying in bed together. She gives him a word and he returns it as a story. She says: "I took that story and wove it into the hem of my nightgown." This is how stories help us grow together.

WEEK 43
Stories are our collective responsibility

 **Think about...**

We think of stories as something personal.

"This is my story," **we say. Or** *"You seem to have a completely different story!"* **Or** *"I wonder what they are saying about this now!"* **Or** *"Her story doesn't fit."* **Of course, each of us has our own experience and our own lens on the world through our stories, but stories exist in a collective space.**

Each of us is a StoryField. We've already explored the intersection of our own personal stories. We are also impacted, and often co-opted, by the stories in the collective field. Stories are meant to be made and shared. Even if you are sitting alone writing, you are still impacted by the stories that surround you.

I spent almost thirty years living in the Southern Hemisphere. I moved to New Zealand when I was twenty-five, so my accent was already set. Even though I'd lived in Europe, spoke fluent German, and had plenty of experience in the world by that time, I still sounded like an American. I began to call *Where are you from?* my "graciousness question."

When I was feeling gracious, I remembered that this question was a way for people to find out about me and to make connection. In both the English-speaking world, and more importantly in the Maori-speaking world, this question is a way to place people within a network of relationship and belonging. However, whenever I could sense that someone was asking me the question to confirm their assumptions about me, I found it deeply annoying. My heritage was attempting to co-opt me into a story not of my choosing.

Each of us is subtly influenced by the stories that circulate around us. Our Western storyline tells us that we need to BE more, HAVE more, DO more. This storyline comes at us through social media, TV and computer screens and publications of all kinds. The focus on success has the subtle (or sometimes not so subtle) underbelly that we are never enough.

Further, it tells us that progress is the answer to every problem. Through an interconnected digital world and the spread of consumerism, this storyline is replicating itself in every society. Not surprisingly, this storyline is damaging the planet and making it very hard to be a well-adjusted young person. The story that I must unceasingly *continue to work on myself* is a subtle form of violence.

Think about the stories that are alive within and around you. Are they truly your own or are they repeated out of habit? For example, if people in your circle continue to tell a certain story about a different group of people, how does your experience compare? Have you sought out and listened to someone from that group? Have you worked with them? Have you asked *them* what it is like to be living *their* life? Much of our prejudice and fear comes from ignorance about the real-life stories of others.

One of the fastest ways to change the story *is* to change the story.

- **What stories do you need to stop telling** because they are no longer helpful or are even downright harmful?
- **What stories do you keep telling** or circulate more widely because they are generative and bring life to us or our community?
- **What stories do you start telling** because they open a doorway to a new possibility, generate more aliveness or illuminate what we can be or do better together?

What could change if YOU (and all of us) started to tell different stories?

Which stories need to change so that we can choose a more flourishing future?

 *Take action...*

What needs changing at home? There is still not a full-scale peace in Northern Ireland, yet things have dramatically shifted. A key component in the shift started at the dinner table. When mothers told their children different stories — and stopped reinforcing the cycle of retaliation and violence — the cycle shifted. *What stories need to change at home?*

What needs changing in the workplace? Although we assume that adults show up at work, many of us are not surprised when we witness behaviors that are surprisingly immature. The behaviors we experienced in the playground are still taking place in the boardroom. We see bullying, dominance, control, the subtle (or not so subtle) violence of force. We tell stories about each other that serve to stereotype or harm. Or maybe we are stuck in the downward spiral of negative storytelling. *What stories need to change in the workplace?*

> One of the fastest ways to change the story **is** to change the story.

What needs changing in the community? Although most of us would say that community is a virtue, many people still feel isolated. It seems hard to make connections. There's too much to pay attention to in our lives. Especially our younger people, who are turning more and more to social media where they experience sound bites and have fewer and fewer true conversations. More aggression is showing up online and is spilling out into the rest of life. It has become ever easier to scapegoat specific groups. *What stories need to change in your community?*

What needs changing in politics? Politicians could be said to be in public service. At least that used to be the intended role of someone in government. It appears that special interest groups have taken over the microphone and more and more stories are being used to put attention on a particular view rather than to gain an overview. *What stories need to change about politics?*

These may appear to be categories that cannot be changed by a single person. But your story and how you choose to tell and hold it can make all the difference.

Awakening to your surroundings and your habits and making a conscious choice is the first step. What stories do we need to STOP telling? What stories do we need to KEEP telling? What stories do we need to START telling?

 Have a look...

The Corrymeela peace centre[49] in Northern Ireland has been dedicated to a new story since it was founded after World War II. Their iceberg model of conflict shows how conflicts escalate and what can help to de-escalate them. This part of the process has been mapped well and they have a solid training process around it. The underside or hidden part of the iceberg, the vast majority of its bulk, are the stories that swirl around the conflict. Often, even though the protagonists have moved into reconciliation, their extended networks are stuck in playing out the old stories of conflict. Only when these shift can real peace come.

What stories will I stop/keep/start telling?

...and why?

PART FOUR

Your Future Story

There is so much trying to influence how we see the world, it can be hard to keep up. At the same time, humans are community creatures; we want to belong. Both of these together make thinking for yourself a subversive act. Where do you need to move away from the shared storyline and create your own?

Every day you have a fundamental choice: *Do you choose to be awake in your life, or not?* The way that stories work in our minds often means that they operate as a rearview mirror and we see the large movements that led to where we are now. But in truth, life is a series of small choices, made in the moment. Each choice adds to our storyline. Whether that storyline feels like a rich one or not depends on these choices and how conscious we are in making them.

When we bring consciousness to the stories we live in, we get to choose how they impact us. Stories are made of moments. What moments are you choosing?

Start by looking for that which makes you feel most alive, most engaged, most on fire. Claim your superpower and tell that story. Cultivate your courage and stamina. Be bold and step into action. Take a closer look at what's transforming within you and what you want to transform. From this vantage point, what's the future story you want to tell?

In these coming weeks we will build a story resource to take you forward. Imagine it as a backpack full of strength, focus and energy you can dig into at any moment. You have the resources you need. They lie in the stories you choose to carry with you.

In **Part 3** we looked at how stories work in the world and how they carry many potent qualities. We took on the role of a **Story Activist** and stepped directly into practice. Now, in **Part 4**, the final part of our work together this year, we return again to ourselves. We put the final foundation in place to create a transformational future, one in which more of the greatest story of *you* can unfold.

WEEK 44
What stories help to resource you?

Think about...

Oh, that sense of being alive in every cell and fiber of your being!

Somehow it gives the world a glow and makes all things seem possible, even in the midst of challenge. When have you felt the rapture of being truly alive? What caused you to feel that way? How can you capture that inside of you now?

Psychologists call this feeling "a resourceful state." And "state" here could be thought of as state of mind or state of being. When negative stories are active, we easily fall into a negative state. Everything feels more constricted. Focusing on possibility and potential creates a constructive state of mind. That doesn't mean you don't see challenges and impediments; you just don't choose to live there.

When you feel alive and present, you also feel more capable and resourceful. You are naturally open to the support and resources in your environment, even if they aren't visible to you yet. You are more open and playful, therefore more creative. You aren't pushed down by circumstance, but can rise to the occasion.

Runners talk of "being in the zone." Basketball players speak of the team somehow operating like one being. Mihaly Csikszentmihalyi[50] — a Hungarian psychologist — recognized and named the psychology of this highly focused mental state, in which time seems to stand still and more can be accomplished. He called it "flow."

Being in the flow is like being a better version of yourself. Capturing the stories of times when you felt most alive, most contributing and most connected to purpose gives you the foundation you need to recreate that state more often. This state is the launching pad for liftoff.

What is your repertoire of resourceful state stories?

> Capturing the stories of times when you felt most alive and most connected to purpose helps you recreate that state more often.

First, be a StoryCatcher for your personal resourceful state stories. Think back through your life and note down moments when you:
- Felt highly alive, engaged, present, contributing.
- Felt working with others was effortless, really productive or downright fun.
- Were in the zone. Hours passed and you suddenly realized that you accomplished more than you dreamed possible.
- Had a sense of delighted discovery.
- Had a sense of childlike wonder or awe.
- Felt creative or full of imagination or ideas came easily to you.
- Felt the support of allies — people, places, circumstances, or even a concept like hope or love.
- Felt as if you took positive leadership for yourself or others.
- Knew yourself to be resourced or resourceful.
- Felt connected to nature or the natural world.

Now, look to others' stories. Search out stories of others who have been passionately, truly alive or those who have accomplished positive things. What can you learn from them?

Take a deeper look at the stories you collected. What conditions made a resourceful state possible? What did you do to make the most of that state?

What did you learn from your story collection that can help you to step into aliveness now? What stories do you want to be sure to carry with you?

 **Have a look...**

Just to remind you of the moments you *do have*. 525,600 minutes every year. Take a look at the opening number of the film version of the musical *RENT*, called "Seasons of Love."[51]

WEEK 45

Which stories remind you to find and follow your bliss?

Think about...

Joseph Campbell was often quoted as saying "follow your bliss."

He wasn't referring to a state of over-happy lethargy, he was referring to that sense of primed and joyful awareness that leads you in new and surprising directions. The bliss he was speaking about is like being tuned into a radio station that keeps leading you forward into the next expression of purposeful life.

When you're following your bliss, even the rocky road can be full of learning. Turning over each stone enables you to see one more piece of the puzzle. In the end, the stones you stumbled over become the bridge to the next level. People who are following their bliss seem to have a glow about them. It feels as if they have an internal booster pack that keeps them going. They are charged up enough to help charge up others.

However, there's a challenge to this way of living. You have to remain curious. You have to become comfortable with the "not-knowing" and be ready to stay in it long enough for the next steps to appear. You have to learn to be still enough to listen to that inner voice of intuition and trust it enough to follow where it wants to lead.

Having a look at stories of following your bliss reminds your heart and mind that you could do it more often.

Just after I left my last full-time job in New Zealand through a legal process, it felt like the world had ended. I decided to take a break in the States, and travel purely on intuition. I would let myself be guided to a place and then ask: *Why am I here?* Usually, within ten minutes someone or something would show up and a new part of the adventure would begin. My story continued to unfold in perfect timing.

What is your bliss? When have you felt a moment or a period of perfect alignment, a time when you said to yourself, "Hey! *This* is what I'm meant to do!" and you followed your conviction? Having a look at your stories of following your bliss reminds your heart and mind that you know how to do this and you could do it more often. Where the heart and mind lead, the rest of you will follow.

What do your stories show you about finding and following your bliss?

Take action...

Once again, scan your life experience. When have you followed your bliss? Think back to those moments in which you felt as if you were on track, on purpose, being led by something greater than yourself, or flowing easily. What was happening? Make some story notes. What do these moments have in common? What do they show you about finding or following your bliss?

When have you felt true appreciation for what life has given you? Think back to those times when you really appreciated what life has given you, both the good and the bad. Perhaps you could see the gift in the situation or find yourself strengthened by the challenge. Maybe you received unexpected kindness or support. What stories help you to capture the sense of true appreciation?

When have you been in the attitude of surrender or deep gratitude for receiving? Rediscover those times when you felt led or supported by something greater than yourself. How did it feel to surrender to the moment or be in service of something beyond yourself? Many people know how to give, but they don't know how to receive. When were the times you were deeply grateful for receiving, when you could really take in the gift you've been given? What can you learn from these stories?

In the book *The More Beautiful World Our Hearts Know is Possible*[52], **author Charles Eisenstein talks a lot about story.** Here's what he says about how story and leadership fit together: *"To be fully in service of something one has experienced as real is the essence of leadership in a nonhierarchical age. A leader is the holder of a story, someone whose experience of its reality is deep enough so that she can hold the belief on behalf of others."*

WEEK 46

How can story help you find and embrace your superpower?

 *Think about...*

Go on, tell us what your superpower is!

And don't think about this flippantly; a superpower is a wonderful thing to have. Clark Kent was a reporter for a newspaper with a power he kept hidden; secretly he was Superman. He was faster than a speeding bullet and able to leap tall buildings in a single bound. Okay, so maybe you can't fly, but Superman's not the only one with a superpower.

Parents seem to birth their superpowers along with their children. Mothers are attuned to their babies, even across town. Some parents really do have eyes in the backs of their heads. Others just seem to know when somebody needs comforting or strong boundaries.

Maybe you have a way of putting people at ease. Perhaps folks tell you their stories or you are the one everyone turns to for help. Maybe you are always standing just at the place where the train doors open (okay, this happens to be one of mine!). Or you have a unique way of viewing the world that helps people see *their* world in a new light.

Maybe you are a person who can make the complex simple or the simple extraordinary. Maybe you can sense into the future like no one else, or you are able to look into the past and search out what is still needed now. *What is it?*

Even though the word *superpower* seems to focus on something big, a superpower can also exist in something that appears ordinary. There are people who transmit love in their cooking. There are those who can uplift your spirits by sitting next to you. Some people have a voice that can transport their listeners.

So when you think about your superpower, think about that thing you are uniquely able to do. Think broadly. A superpower is rarely something that shows up on your resumé, but it can make all the difference! Find out what it is and let it become part of your story. As Sinead McKeough once said: "Peddle your oddities like precious commodities." The things you can uniquely do set you apart from anyone else. They give you special capacities that might be life changers for other people.

Where can the story of your secret superpower come alive?

Time for a brainstorm! What are all the quirky, strange, wonderful, challenging, unique things you can do? Make them into a mind map or a picture or turn them into a three-dimensional version of your brainstorm. When you look at them in this form, what do you see? How are they connected? What do they enable you to do that others cannot?

Ask friends, family and colleagues to chime in. What do they think your superpower is?

Take it further. Which of these capacities gives you joy? Or is even a "guilty pleasure"? Where can you expand on the talents you already have? Maybe you're a bookaholic who just loves reading. Can you turn this superpower into a new story for yourself? Could people order a bibliophile's astrology reading from you? Could they ask you to go to a nearby bookshop or visit an online book retailer and make a personalized reading list? Can you support children in learning to be excited by reading or encourage someone into literacy?

Make up a story about your superpower. Use the form of a fairytale or another kind of story and focus on your superpower. What happens to the you in this story because of this superpower? What happens to others? What ideas does that give you?

 Have a look...

The Greatest Showman is the story of P.T. Barnum and the crew of amazing individuals he recruited to become part of his show. A lot of dedication and love[53] went into making this movie and it shines through. In the song *This is Me*[54], the performers claim their place as exactly who they are. This movie carries a warning, though; it has a soundtrack so good that it might be on permanent repeat in your head.

> A superpower can make all the difference! Find out what it is and let it become part of your story.

WEEK 47
What story will keep you going no matter what?

 **Think about...**

Perseverance demands stamina.

This is not the burst of speed a sprinter puts on, but the kind of stamina you need to keep going over time, especially when the goal is much larger than you are. A marathon runner knows that pacing is key. This is the skill of running many small races that add up to a big one.

Elizabeth Gilbert, author of *Big Magic*[55], often talks about the stamina it takes to be an author. She says that the ancient Greeks had it right about the quality of genius. They didn't believe that genius resided *inside* a person. Rather that the person had to act in such a way that genius was attracted to come to them. They believed genius was a co-creation. Gilbert says that the biggest part of being an author is the commitment to keep showing up and keep writing.

The advice to simply keep going no matter what is particularly valuable, whether you're having amazing success or suffering a devastating failure. After a failure, it takes courage and a big dollop of perseverance to step back up and try again. And strangely enough, it is even more challenging to create in the wake of a success. You might wonder if you can ever do such a thing again. But you're not the only one wondering. The pressure of expectation can be extreme.

One way to keep your practice going is simply to keep practicing. If you're a runner, keep running. If you're a dancer, keep dancing (and have a look at the movie *Inside I'm Dancing* for inspiration). If you're a lover, keep loving. Do these things no matter how the form changes, simply being committed to learning for the learning's sake.

Take all these things you're learning and weave them into a story that can help you when times get tough. Find the story that will support you to just take the next step, no matter what.

What story of perseverance can help you keep going through the ups and downs of life?

What does perseverance mean to you? Take some time to really think about it. What would you name this quality for yourself? My SHOW UP AND DO IT-NESS? 150% commitment? "No matter what"? Having your own phrase or motto is a great reminder. Write your word or phrase onto a sticky note and post it in a prominent place.

What are the principles you want to take into life with you to help you keep going? Colleagues of mine have the principle "leave beauty in your wake." With this they acknowledge that things won't always be perfect and that sometimes the work needs to happen at speed, but there can still be beauty.

A couple I knew had "assume love-acious intent" as one of their principles[56]. You know malicious intent, right? That means someone intends to do you harm. They made up the word "love-acious" to remind themselves that the other person had love as their intention, they just might not have done a very good job expressing it. What are your principles?

Whose stamina and perseverance do you admire? (Maybe even your own?) Gather some stories that can be fuel when you need them.

 ## Have a look...

I was living in New Zealand when the Lord of the Rings movies were being filmed. I've seen them all multiple times, watching for people I know, places I've been and finally for the story itself. One of my favorite scenes in the third movie, *Return of the King*, is the lighting of the beacon fires[57].

There are many things to notice about this scene. First, the elder must stand back and play the support role as the apprentice goes to light the beacon. Gandalf is not the prime mover in this scene; the hobbit Pippin is. He needs to overcome his own lack of self-confidence to step up to this responsibility. He's very pleased with the results until he notices he's actually standing in the fire!

Then the beacons are lit in rapid succession. But think a moment — how long did the watchers need to wait on top of the mountains for their role to be needed? It must have felt like forever. They had to keep the faith. They had to persevere so they were ready when their time eventually came.

Finally Aragorn rushes into the hall shouting: *"The beacon fires are lit! Gondor calls for aid!"* There is a long, seemingly unending, and uncomfortable silence. Will anyone answer the call? This is what it feels like when you can see what is needed for the present or the future, but others have yet to understand your point of view. Can you persevere? Finally, King Théoden responds: *"And Rohan will answer!"* The final movement in a long series of adventures and trials begins.

WEEK 48
How can stories impact your choices for the better?

 **Think about...**

Life is so many tiny choices.

Do I turn left or right? Should I speak to the stranger next to me? Am I committed enough to exercise each morning? Do I entertain this thought? If you've ever wondered, "How did I get here?" then you've probably realized how much courage it can take to trace the pathway. One choice after the other, building on each other, and life takes on a certain momentum. Soon the pathway seems set in stone.

Consider for a moment, though, that choice, and therefore life, is malleable. If life is made up of moments and each moment is made up of choices, then you really do create your own life. Even when all other choices are removed, you have the choice of how you respond to this moment.

That's what Viktor Frankl[58] discovered in the concentration camp at Auschwitz during World War II. As a psychologist, he wondered who would survive such a horrific experience. He began to notice those around him. There were those who came from privileged backgrounds and much advantage; there were those who were physically strong or morally upright. But he found those who survived were not the strongest or the most advantaged. Those who survived had a purpose greater than the suffering they were experiencing.

> **What small, but maybe bold, or even crazy, choice can you make in this moment that could change everything?**

He also determined that he would survive. He began to realize that hate is more of a prison than the one he was experiencing. His book *Man's Search for Meaning* further developed his "logotherapy" and identified some important attributes of choices that create more humanity. He explored how even suffering can have meaning.

You may never be faced with the kind of experiences he had, but you have the same power of choice in every moment. How will you choose to respond to what's in front of you? What small, but maybe bold, or even *crazy*, choice can you make in this moment — *the unexpected choice* — that could change everything?

What stories are guiding your choices and what choices are guiding your stories?

 Take action...

Have a look at your palette of choices. There are choices in every moment. Which ones are you aware of? Could you slow down, take a breath and be more conscious about them? Could you eat more slowly? Walk more slowly? Give yourself a stillness break? Make the call you've been putting off? Choose to look at your resistance? Mend the bridge to a friend? Especially where you have the feeling you have no choice, can you consider that maybe you do?

Take a look at your choice habits. What kind of choices do you make easily? What do you normally do when faced with a difficult choice? Is that a helpful behavior? What choices do you make about your attitude? How conscious are you around choice and choices?

What are your stories around choice? Everything that happens is a space/time event. We are the ones who make meaning around the happenings. Sometimes in defining meaning around a happening, our stories can be helpful. Sometimes they can keep us stuck. We can get invested in a meaning we've created and that meaning can keep us feeling small or broken or that someone else has all the power. Where do your stories need to shift in order for you to feel you have choice?

 Have a look...

What would it be like to live your life totally the way you want it?
Miriam and Peter Lancewood[59] chose to leave consumer society and live in the New Zealand bush. They bathed in the stream, hunted in the forest and fended for themselves. It is a bold choice. Perhaps you don't want to go bush, but what is *your* bold choice? Where are you prepared to change your story and take a risk?

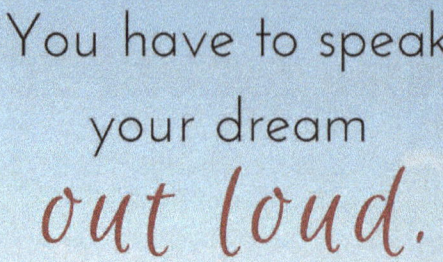

You have to speak your dream *out loud.*

KELLY CORRIGAN

WEEK 49
What stories can bring your dream to life?

 **Think about...**

Everyone has a dream.

Some dreams are loud and colorful and out-there. They attract attention because of their very audacity. Some are quiet and unassuming, below the radar. Maybe they went underground because they had to in order to survive. Their owner might think they are dead and gone, but they found a tiny corner of the heart to hide in. And some appear to be like Sleeping Beauty, cursed never to awaken unless just the right conditions appear.

Do you remember your long-ago dreams? When you were young, did you dream of making a difference or being famous? Did you want to excel at a sport or an art? Maybe you longed for a family, dreamed of having a child or loved animals so much that others accused you of starting a zoo.

Perhaps your dream was to write a great novel or be a scientist. Maybe you dreamed of leading your country or finding a cure for the disease that claimed someone you loved. Did you long for travel or adventure? Maybe you still do.

Dreams are important for our health. Imagination is one of the greatest gifts of humanity and everyone has it. When we are children, playing with imagination is what we most love to do. As adults, we are encouraged to turn our focus to the "real world." We are told to stifle our imaginations or at least to quiet them down. Yet everything that exists was once a dream, a product of the imagination. That's why it is vitally important to cultivate the imagination and use it whenever you can. You might just be holding the key for something humanity desperately needs at this time.

Playing with story is a quick way to reach the imagination, because in a story, anything is possible. You can awaken your long-ago dream and experience it. You can dream a new dream and make it come to life. Working with stories is a way to dream your dream out loud and be in action for its future.

What dream can your stories bring to life?

> In a story, anything is possible. Working with stories is a way to dream your dream out loud and be in action for its future.

What is your dream? Use old magazines, pictures, paper and the colors of your choice to make a collage of your dream or create it digitally. It doesn't matter whether this dream is an old one or one that's appearing right now. The main thing is that your heart takes a leap when you think about it. Use all the materials you have available to make your dream a visual reality.

Now create stories about your dream. Create a different story each day about some aspect of the dream. You might be the lead character in your story or maybe you want to choose another character as your alter ego. Be truthful: who have you always wanted to be? Choose that one as the star of the stories. Let your imagination free and see what unfolds during the week your dream is allowed to grow through your storytelling.

Read your stories out loud. You don't necessarily need an audience, but having someone else listen is helpful. It gives your imagination the attention it needs to get even more creative.

 **Have a look...**

Making something visible means that it can manifest. Have a look at Patti Dobrowolski's[60] TED Talk about drawing your life and see how it works. Give it a try!

WEEK 50

How can your story empower you to act?

 **Think about...**

Dr. Martin Luther King Jr. had something quite significant to say about love and power.

"Power without love is reckless and abusive, and love without power is sentimental and anemic," he said. He shows us in this statement that love and power were not meant to act alone. They were actually meant to dance together.

Power, in this sense, is a noun that needs to be qualified. It isn't good or bad; it derives its value from how it is used. This is the same for anything you can use powerfully. A little rain is beneficial; way too much rain is a flood. A bulldozer can be used to clear a space for a garden, or it can be used to tear something down under protest. Leadership can stimulate or it can stifle. It depends on how it is used.

Love, in the context of Dr. King's words, is a verb. When it is merely a concept, is it weak and ineffective, a cotton candy of a thing that disappears under too much pressure. But when it is enacted powerfully, love can move mountains and it can move people into positive change.

Where are you prepared to put the story of your life and your contribution to the world into action?

Dr. King goes on: "Power at its best is love implementing the demands of justice, and justice at its best is power correcting everything that stands against love." When these two work together, power is tempered by love, and love is powerful in action.

Sometimes we can lack both courage and agency in the areas where we know we need to act. We are afraid of how things might turn out or fearful even to begin. This is where stories can help to give us backbone and willingness.

Where are you prepared to put the story of your life and your contribution to the world into action? As David Whyte says in his poem "Start Close In"[61], the first step you need to take is the one closest to you, the one you are most afraid of.

What will your stories help you do?

Take action...

Ponder your relationship to love and power. What have you learned or experienced in your life about these two, both separately and together? If love and power were people, how would you describe your relationship to each one of them? What about their relationship to each other? What could be done to create a strong, healthy relationship with these two?

How do love and power work in your world? What experiences have you had with love and power at home and at work? In your culture? In your extended family or your religious or spiritual practice? What are the stories that perpetuate how these two are practiced around you? Can you "listen them out" and identify them?

What new story will you tell about your own love and power? What story will help you to claim (or even reclaim) your personal practice of love and power? Create one or more stories that will help you remember the relationship you'd like to forge with these two great forces.

 **Have a look...**

The video for Sara Bareilles's song *Brave*[62] always makes me smile. Where are you willing to dance like no one's watching? When will you be willing to make your dream come true?

WEEK 51
What story can help you transform?

 *Think about...*

There are so many ways you can give a gift to the world, but one of the most personal, perhaps the most intimate, is by sharing your story.

With each story you tell you are building a picture of yourself and how you operate in the world. Piece by piece, line by line, you are making the creation of your Self. In this creation you have great power. You have the power of how you choose to see things.

You are unique in the way you see and make meaning of things. You might have grown up in the same house as someone else, you might have been part of the same trauma, you might have lived through the same devastating or amazing experience and yet your take on it will be your own.

It is a powerful stance to consciously choose what your experience will mean. In fact, *everything depends on it*. Was it a failure or another learning experience? Was it a premeditated act or was someone calling for help? Can you see beyond the difference to find the bridge?

As we tell our story, we begin to create a pathway for our thoughts and attention. First it is a small track, barely visible in the jungle of the mind. With more elaboration it becomes an established trail and further on a super highway, with thoughts and actions flowing along in lightning speed. The more we tell a story, the truer it becomes for us.

Here's where the power of listeners comes in. With the focus of someone else's attention, our stories can shift and change. They transform in the crucible of attention. Be your own best listener. Listen deeply to the younger you who made meaning. Work with them on the new meaning you choose for that experience. Right now, *in this very moment*, you have the opportunity to change your life. Will you take it?

Where is your story transforming right now? Where is a story transforming you?

Take one of your most-told stories from childhood. Pretend you are picking it up, like an object. In fact, you see it is a kaleidoscope, with many colors and fractal patterns. Have a look through this kaleidoscope of story and choose a different view. What does the story sound like from the perspective of another person who was there? What does it sound like if you told it from the view of place, as if place were telling the story? What if you chose to tell it from another perspective, like the perspective of love or relationship or history? How does this transform how you see this story? What do you see as a result?

Where can you spot the need for transformation? Where are there stuck stories in your life, perhaps stories you sense are leading you to a dead end or the same pothole in the road you continue to fall into? Try taking them apart. Look at each part of the story, instead of the rush to conclusion or naming the trauma or limitation. Where can you stretch or magnify part of the story? Where can you minimize parts? If you would tell it with a different and more transformative end, what would that sound like?

Where can the story lead? If you were holding an intention to tell the most powerful, transformative story of your life you possibly could, what would it sound like? Go on and tell it. Really! *I dare you!* See what happens if you keep telling it for some time.

 Have a look…

One of my favorite movies of all time is a Swedish film called *As It Is in Heaven.* It is the story of a world-famous conductor who has lived in the rarified bubble of music but who doesn't really know how to live in the world. Diagnosed with a heart condition, he returns to his childhood village and there faces the ghosts of the past in such a way that it transforms all the people around him. In *Gabriella's Song*[63], one of the main characters learns to stand up and claim her place and her power.

> Stories transform in the crucible of attention. Be your own best listener.

You don't just have a story - *you're a Story in the making,* and you never know what the next chapter's going to be. That's what makes it exciting.

DAN MILLMAN

WEEK 52
What is your story in the making?

Think about...

What kind of story have you decided to live in?

Is it an adventure? A hero's tale? A love story? The unfolding of a myth in modern times? It might be a story that is told for generations to come or it may be that kind of quiet tale that those who know you share on cold and wintery nights to warm their souls and keep them going.

Who can tell what your story might become and what you might face in the future? But we do know this: the story you are living *in* is often the story you are living *into*. If your story is too small for you, if it is limiting you, if it is paining you, then the person to change it is YOU.

Storymaking is like any other practice — *it takes practice*. That means it also takes commitment, attention and a good serving of curiosity. The desire for something, even the *love* of something, is needed if you want to become masterful in it. A friend of mine once described being present at a rarely-performed Zen Buddhist ceremony in Japan. The master of the temple ran through the assembly and leapt onto a raised platform. In the midst of performing a somersault he shot an arrow into the center of the waiting target. This takes more than skill. It takes becoming one with the arrow *and* the target so that they find each other perfectly in the moment.

In essence, you and your story are one. If you are not the master of your story, then you are simply an extension of it, continuing down a certain track. But when you master your story, it is an extension of you and you can watch it unfold, in wonder and delight. Which do you choose?

What is your story in the making?

Take time to look back. Have a look over the journey. What were the high points? The low or challenging points? What were the notes you took about what you wanted to remember? Where have you taken new steps or evolved new ways of being or acting? How do you feel about your story now and in what ways are you living it? Make some journey notes now. And figure out a great way to celebrate yourself. *WELL DONE!*

What is your sense of your unfolding story now? Considering all that you've experienced in our time together, what are the fruits you are now ready to pick? What are the new shoots coming up through the soil? And what are the seeds that are now ready to germinate? What have you learned about being a story gardener?

Write a letter to your future self. Tell this future self your intention for the coming time and how you see your story unfolding. Do you have a wish or a blessing for your future self? Write it in the letter. Seal it and either put it away or ask a friend to send it to you in three, six or twelve months' time.

Have a look...

Have a look, once more, at yourself in the mirror. How have you changed during this journey we've been on? What can you now see and appreciate about yourself? What do you want to honor or affirm? Where do you want to give yourself courage and strength? Look into the mirror and speak the words you've been waiting to hear.

> When you master your story, it is an extension of you and you can watch it unfold, in wonder and delight.

Insights and gifts from the journey

Share your treasures with the 365 ALIVE! Community

Act as if
what you do
makes a difference.
It does.

WILLIAM JAMES

REMEMBER—

Your story matters!

Congratulations!
YOU MADE IT!

You've spent a whole year focusing on the core of what matters — the stories that support you to be *you*. You have investigated how stories work in the world and the stories at work in *your* world. Whether you realized it or not, you have been living the storyteller's life — you *are* a storyteller. That means there's both good news and bad news. The bad news is: *Things will never be the same again*. The good news is: *Things will never be the same again*[64].

It is certainly true that when you know someone's story, you can never see them the same way you did before. Now that you have delved deeply into story, how you see others has changed. Perhaps this has also happened inside you. Knowing your own stories helps you see yourself in a new light. Therefore, be gentle with yourself, and kind to others. Now that you know about what story can do, use it wisely.

The purpose of focusing on stories is to wake up to the power they have in your life and to take that power back. Becoming awake to your stories means that you have the choice to stay aware and to be active in shaping the stories that shape you.

We have been on what I call a "figure-eight" journey, first outwards, then inwards in order to go outwards and then inwards again. You've taken a deep dive into the weaving of story in your own life, had a look at how stories work in the world then returned to your own ground to see what story you wanted to create for the future.

Across these fifty-two weeks we've explored many facets of story:
- How they work inside of us and pattern the way we respond to the world
- How we are each a StoryField, the intersection of stories we hold about ourselves and all the stories held about us by others, including our family and cultural structures, and beyond
- How beginning to work with different aspects of a story changes it, sometimes in subtle ways and sometimes in large ways
- How stories can divide us or make a bridge, how they can create empathy and understanding if we choose to be open to them
- How emotional resilience and curiosity are needed to stand in the fire of stories, both our own and others'
- How we are creating the pathway we walk each day through the stories we pay attention to

Now it's up to you. You have the awareness and the tools to make a difference with your stories. How will you decide to continue your story practice? It is my hope and my dream that you have come to a deeper knowledge both about yourself and your story, and that you continue down the road as journey companions. Bringing more life to your stories brings more interesting stories into your life.

THANK YOU for being on this journey with me! I'd love to hear what happened for you — what you've seen, what you've learned and what you've decided to do as a result. If you feel inspired, please drop me a line and share your stories.

Wishing you good storymaking!

EPILOGUE

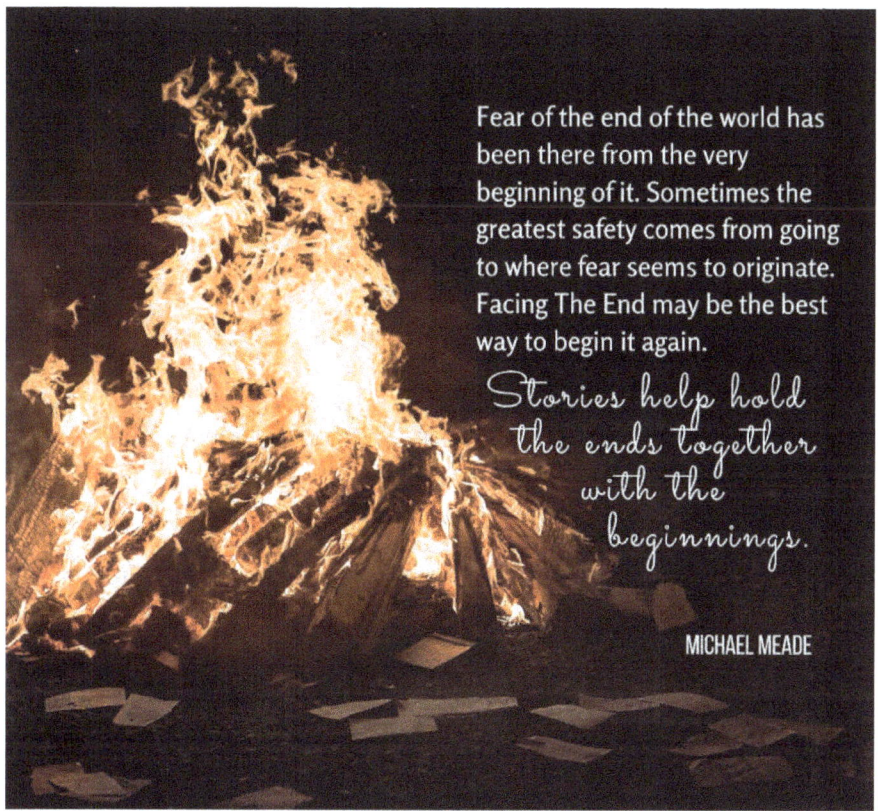

Fear of the end of the world has been there from the very beginning of it. Sometimes the greatest safety comes from going to where fear seems to originate. Facing The End may be the best way to begin it again.

Stories help hold the ends together with the beginnings.

— MICHAEL MEADE

I finished writing the body of this book almost exactly a year ago.

At that point I stopped focusing on it and took up my life on the road again. My suitcase and I became constant companions as I worked and journeyed my way through places I know, with people I love, in Europe, Australia, New Zealand and Canada.

As I landed back at home again in early 2020, I was already beginning to plan the year ahead. The calendar was full of travel and interesting engagements. I would once again be circling the globe and contributing story and hosting to a wide variety of projects and groups. There were conversations to have and travels to plan. Even at that moment, though, something was changing.

I had been feeling the deep personal call to go inward, be silent and let a new story arise. This call had already come like a soft tug on my sleeve and it held the whisper of creativity and promise. It danced on the edge of my busy-ness. But as any good story will tell you, a promise like this is made at the crossroads. A crossroads indicates that something new is coming, and also that something must be left behind. Usually, there is quite a journey even to get to the crossroads.

The journey came in a way I could have least expected. This time evolution signaled itself both on the personal level and for humanity as a whole. COVID-19 appeared first on the horizon and then spread like wildfire around the world. As a narrative practitioner, I reflected that this is the first time that *all of us*, every single member of humanity, have been part of the same story in the same moment.

In an attempt to contain the spread, many nations went into lockdown. The virus sent us home. So what does *home* mean from a story point of view?

To return home means to return to the hearth, the central fire of your upbringing. At the deepest level, it is an invitation to revisit your founding story. Where do I come from? Who are my people? What is their legacy? It is a call to revisit tribal truths and family values and to sift through them to see what is still relevant now and what is no longer useful.

We have had time to wonder what makes a home and how we behave at home. We've had time to see our family patterns and what we've forgotten about being a family in our rush to join the consumer society. We have been forced to take on roles we had allocated to others, as school came to the kitchen table and elders needed support and supplies. We shared our personal spaces and lives as children and animals made their presence known in business meetings.

We saw a massive explosion of creativity as people began to cope with a new daily storyline. Suddenly habits were interrupted and people experimented and shared what they learned. We played and laughed together over distance.

People found each other and reconnected. We learned how to celebrate and touch in new ways. And we learned how to grieve as the losses began to be felt.

Coming home meant we've had time to experience what secrets might come to light when we are forced into close proximity. Some people have learned to explore the new territories of each other with renewed curiosity. And some people have been forced to reflect on their own inner worlds. Old stories asked for attention. Secrets that are dark and dangerous came to the surface. Individual and collective trauma began to play itself out.

We found out what it means to be neighbors when we began once again to look after each other, or saw where no one cared. We were confronted with

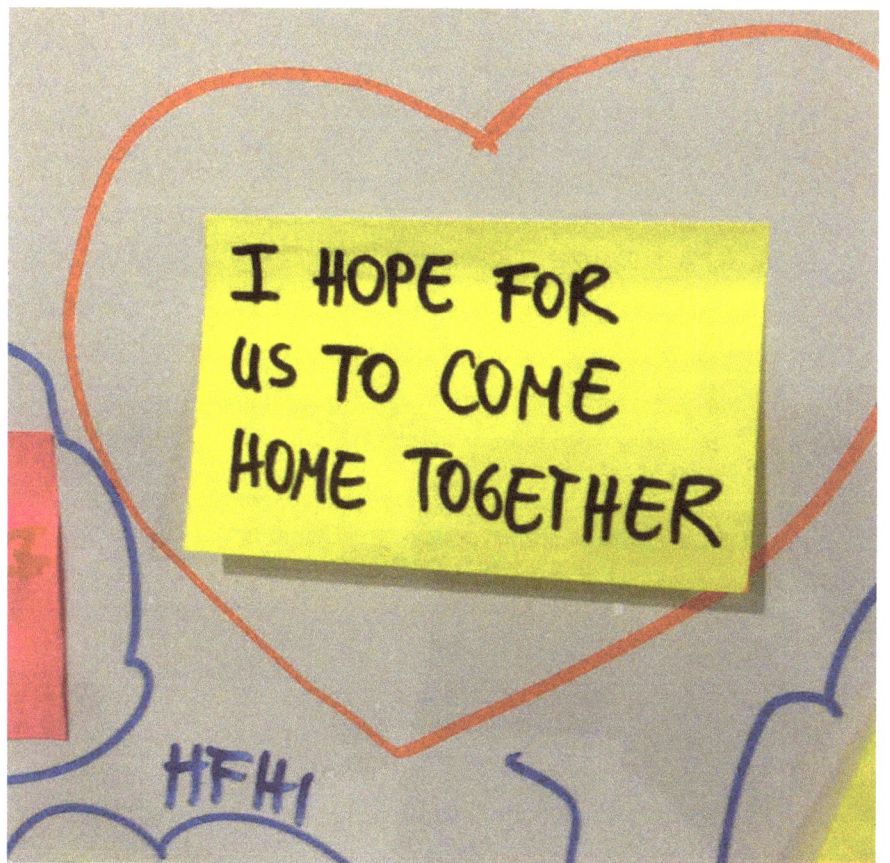

the obsession to look and where we had also obsessively chosen not to see. Eight minutes and forty-six seconds of violence[66] ignited the need for a new level of conversation about coming home together. It also showed how much further we have to go as people, as nations and as a world.

As I sit in this evolutionary crux point, I can hear ever more clearly the call to attend to story. This moment asks us to be even more awake to the inherent power of stories and to be conscious about the stories we decide to live with, create and share. It calls us to become cognizant of the stories we are unconsciously living in and to ask whether they serve life. Instead of trying to return to what was once "normal" or to rush headlong into the next idea of what might be, the world invited us to push the PAUSE button. It invites us to reconsider every story of who we think we are and who we might be together.

This is a time to turn to that powerful partner of story, *listening*, and to its elder expression, witnessing. I've always loved the Chinese character Ting, which we translate into English as "to listen." All Hanzi are symbolic pictorial representations of a composite of meanings. This character has within it the concepts of "ears," "undivided attention," "king," "one thousand," and "heart"[67]. Together, these point to the ramifications of the skill of great listening. Something shifts when you treat someone as an honored person; one who is respected. And when you offer attention for a long enough time, the ears become both an outlet for, and a conduit to, the heart. I've learned in my work that it is possible to listen a greater story out of someone than they ever knew they were capable of telling.

When we open our hearts and minds and offer up our attention and listening, we come into the stance of witness. The practice of with-ness-ing[68] means to surrender our own point of view for a time to fully stand with the other and inhabit their world. Before we can tell a new story, we need to witness its beginnings into being. As a human race, we are standing at the crossroads together, a liminal place that Otto Scharmer describes as the bottom of the U, where letting go gives way to letting come. The process of Theory U[69] includes the practice of deep listening and sensing into what is, in order to move through it and discover what might be.

This step necessitates letting go of control. It requires that we put down the old story and stand apart from it for a moment, like a traveler who puts down a bundle and looks at it dispassionately and with clear eyes. Those who say *that's just how it is* have forgotten the millions of tiny decisions, the thousands of actions, the hundreds of stories that made the meaning of today. They forget that we live in a story, and that means we can change it. But first we must be willing to entertain the not-knowing, the feeling adrift, the confusion that indicates the messy middle is here. We have to agree to be in the womb of creation once more and claim ourselves as co-creators. We have to be willing to receive.

What feels like the end times is also the beginning of something new. We are part of a never-ending story[70] that only needs our imagination to live and be expressed in new ways. I believe stories are the library of humanity and we have hidden everything we've ever known in them, as well as in our poems, our songs and our art. Somewhere we've lost the key to meaning, but we can find it again, because we are the legacy of so many storytellers. The important thing to consider is where we invest our time in this library, and how we decide to discover and focus on the wisdom that might be found there. It is time to stop borrowing stories from the FEAR shelf and move into the generative reference section. What stories will we choose to live into and how might these stories truly nourish our evolution? This is a choice each of us can make. You don't need a library card. The barcode to borrow from our human history is located inside you — it's in your DNA.

These are challenging times and yet I feel hopeful. I can sense the light of the fire we've gathered around for eons. It is burning still. I can hear the murmur of voices, the sound of the soup being stirred and the welcome to the weary traveler. I can sense how our future story is calling us into becoming it. This is a journey we are all called to make, alone, and together. I'm waiting at that fire and staring into the flames, where the possibility of my own new story is springing to life, and where I can sense others gathering. We are warming our hands, and our hearts, gathering up courage to make the next round of our journey together.

As I'm sitting on the grass behind my house writing, high above a hawk is making circles in the bright blue of the sky. It calls me to the largest view possible, the bird's-eye view of a planet that is, in the end, a oneness. Suddenly, I see a flash of crimson and a cardinal comes to sit on the wires directly above me, singing. He is a perfect demonstration of being exactly who he is in this moment, a celebration of being alive. I begin to consider that even though he is in my garden, I am part of his territory. We are overlapping circles of life, but I'm the one holding the story. And I'm the one who will decide what to do with it.

Mary Alice Arthur
August 2, 2020

WELCOME TO *365 ALIVE!*

[1] For me, *agency* is not only the ability to take action, but the belief my action is possible and it matters.

[2] Paul Costello, www.storywise.com

PART ONE: GETTING STARTED WITH STORY

[3] I define StoryField as the intersection of all the stories you hold about yourself and others hold about you, as well as the stories that claim and influence you in the form of ancestry, race, gender, ethnicity, place, experience, practice, community, society and popular culture. I originally learned about this concept through a conference hosted by Tom Atlee (https://co-intelligence.org/tomatleebio.html), Peggy Holman (https://peggyholman.com) and others in August 2007 called The Story Field Conference. Peggy Holman wrote about the impact of that event in the February 2008 issue of *AI Practitioner*. Many of my deeper thoughts about this concept came out of conversations held in 2009 at Axladitsa-Avatakia in Greece hosted by Maria Scordialos (https://www.mariascordialos.com) and Sarah Whiteley (https://sarahwhiteley.org), Vanessa Reid (http://www.vanessareid.ca) and others.

[4] Nat Kendall-Taylor, TED talk, *How Words Change Minds: The Science of Storytelling*: https://www.youtube.com/watch?v=Y8wol2nGSpY

[5] Thank you to Petra Sammer for this walk through the history of the visual: www.petrasammer.com

[6] Yep, Paul Costello, again!

[7] Chimamanda Ngozi Adichie, TED talk, *The Danger of a Single Story*: https://www.youtube.com/watch?v=D9Ihs241zeg

PART TWO: MAPPING YOUR PERSONAL STORYFIELD

[8] The term "red thread" actually comes from the British Navy. A colored thread was woven into navy ropes to help identify them. When we speak of a "red thread" in story terms, we mean something that holds a narrative together and gives it sense.

[9] *Powers of Ten*: https://www.youtube.com/watch?v=0fKBhvDjuy0

[10] Jill Bolte Taylor, *My Stroke of Insight*, Viking, 2006.

[11] *The New York Times, Wright's Law: A Unique Teacher Imparts Real Life Lessons*: https://www.youtube.com/watch?v=9bSu_SnIbsw

[12] Storyline Online: *Someone Loves You, Mr. Hatch,* read by Hector Elizondo: https://www.youtube.com/watch?v=AGAS_Aj85cA and *To Be a Drum*, read by James Earl Jones: https://www.youtube.com/watch?v=7BVBBe56MUg

[13] The Rescued Film Project: https://www.youtube.com/watch?v=_I4o_aflTKg

[14] Laurie Lee, *Cider with Rosie*, Hogarth Press, 1959.

[15] Upworthy, "J.K. Rowling found out her books helped save this baby's life. Her response was magic": https://www.upworthy.com/jk-rowling-found-out-her-books-helped-save-this-babys-life-her-response-was-magic?c=ufb3

[16] Job, Joris & Marieke: *A Single Life:* https://vimeo.com/channels/staffpicks/225249697

[17] Dr. Belisa Vranich, *Soldiers use this breathing technique to stay calm:* https://www.youtube.com/watch?v=AO4jxIpw0Rk

[18] Adam Driver, TED talk, *My Journey From Marine to Actor:* https://www.youtube.com/watch?v=nCwwVjPNIoY

[19] Andrew Solomon, TED talk, *How the Worst Moments In Our Lives Make Us Who We Are:* https://www.youtube.com/watch?v=RiM5a-vaNkg

[20] Caroline McHugh, TED talk, *The Art of Being Yourself:* https://www.youtube.com/watch?v=veEQQ-N9xWU

[21] Factory Fifteen, *Robot & Scarecrow:* https://vimeo.com/220442625

[22] Mandy Harvey on America's Got Talent: https://www.youtube.com/watch?v=m9_rtzO3JfY

[23] Warner Brothers, *Ready Player One*, Trailer: https://www.youtube.com/watch?v=cSp1dM2Vj48

[24] New Line Cinema, *The Fellowship of the Ring* — The Council of Elrond: https://www.youtube.com/watch?v=TrJJ6ncp1fc

[25] Arun Maira, "How do we know that our life's work is really done?": https://www.foundingfuel.com/article/how-do-we-know-that-our-lifes-work-is-really-done/

[26] Antoine de Saint-Exupéry, *Le Petit Prince,* Gallimard, 1943.

[27] Bill Nye, *The Science Versus Comedy Tug-of-war That Defines My Career:* https://www.linkedin.com/pulse/bill-nye-science-vs-comedy-tug-of-war-defines-my-career-bill-nye?articleId=6291272998452371456#comments-6291272998452371456&trk=public_profile_article_view

PART THREE: STORY AT WORK IN THE WORLD

[28] "StoryCatcher" is a term coined by Christina Baldwin in her book of the same title. *Storycatcher: Making Sense of Our Lives Through the Power and Practice of Story,* New World Library, 2005.

29. A question asked by Charles Eisenstein in his interview with Oprah Winfrey, OWN, July 16, 2017.
30. *Inclusion Starts With I:* https://www.youtube.com/watch?v=2g88Ju6nkcg
31. Vox: *How Sign Language Innovators Are Bringing Music to the Deaf:* https://www.youtube.com/watch?v=EuD2iNVMS_4
32. Newsner, *Man's Home Is a Haven For Dying Kids:* https://en.newsner.com/family/man-s-home-is-a-haven-for-dying-kids-over-80-children-died-there-already/
33. Robert Waldinger, TED talk, *What Makes A Good Life? Lessons from the longest study on happiness:* https://www.youtube.com/watch?v=8KkKuTCFvzl
34. Thordis Elva & Tom Stranger, TED talk, *Our Story of Rape and Reconciliation:* https://www.youtube.com/watch?v=gyPoqFcvt9w
35. The storyteller was Maria Scordialos from Athens, Greece and the platform was an online series I hosted in 2015 called "People on the Move." https://www.mariascordialos.com
36. *Nineteen Paper Cranes:* https://www.youtube.com/watch?v=s2hpNbELFHo
37. Free Listening Project: https://urbanconfessional.org/join
38. Read about Carl Sagan here: https://en.wikipedia.org/wiki/Carl_Sagan
39. Adam Kahane, *Power and Love: A Theory and Practice of Social Change,* Berrett-Koehler 2011.
40. Emily Wong, *Such Is Life:* https://vimeo.com/207507432
41. Michael Ende, *Momo,* K. Thienemanns Verlag, 1973.
42. J.R.R. Tolkien, *The Lord of the Rings,* Allen & Unwin, 1954.
43. Barry Brailsford, *Song of Waitaha: Histories of a Nation,* Wharariki Publishing Company, 2006.
44. J.K. Rowling, The *Harry Potter* series, Bloomsbury Publishing.
45. BBC, "How Harry Potter became a rallying cry": http://www.bbc.com/culture/story/20180326-the-links-between-harry-potter-and-millennial-protest
46. Southeast Asia Globe, "Thais 'cast a spell' for democracy in Harry Potter-theme protest," https://southeastasiaglobe.com/harry-potter-protest-thailand/
47. Barry Lopez: *Crow and Weasel,* North Point Press, 1990.
48. Elizabeth Gilbert: *Eat, Pray, Love,* Riverhead Books, 2007; *Committed: A Love Story,* Bloomsbury, 2010.
49. Corrymeela Community: https://www.corrymeela.org

PART FOUR: YOUR FUTURE STORY

50. Mihaly Csikszentmihalyi, *Flow: The Psychology of Optimal Experience*, HarperCollins, 2008.
51. Columbia, *RENT*, "Seasons of Love": https://www.youtube.com/watch?v=UvyHuse6buY
52. Charles Eisenstein, *The More Beautiful World Our Hearts Know is Possible*, North Atlantic Books, 2013.
53. 20th Century Fox, *The Greatest Showman*, "From Now On": https://www.youtube.com/watch?v=PluaPvhklMU
54. 20th Century Fox, *The Greatest Showman*, "This is Me": https://www.youtube.com/watch?v=5_WzSbi8aR8
55. Elizabeth Gilbert, *Big Magic*, Riverhead Books, 2015.
56. Thank you to Leanne Babcok for this story!
57. New Line Cinema, *Return of the King*, "Lighting of the Beacons": https://www.youtube.com/watch?v=QhRFaY8A9cA
58. Viktor Frankl, *Man's Search for Meaning*, originally published in 1946.
59. Television New Zealand report, "This couple have spent seven years in the New Zealand wilderness": https://www.youtube.com/watch?v=PHf5p19-Cys
60. Patti Dobrowolski, TED talk, *Draw your future - Take control of your life*: https://www.youtube.com/watch?v=4vl6wCiUZYc
61. David Whyte, "Start Close In": https://pathwriter.wordpress.com/2012/03/19/start-close-in-david-whyte/
62. Sara Bareilles, *Brave*: https://www.youtube.com/watch?v=QUQsqBqxoR4
63. Sonet Film, *As It Is in Heaven* (Sweden, 2014), "Gabriella's Song": https://www.youtube.com/results?search_query=gabriella%27s+song+as+it+is+in+heaven

REMEMBER — YOUR STORY MATTERS!

64. This is a very old story form. One person tells about an event that just happened and the other person says: "Hey, that's bad!" to which the first replies "No, it's good!" and so on. The more you work with stories, the more you will learn that gold can be buried in the deepest dross. Sometimes you just need help finding it. Things will never be the same again.

EPILOGUE

65   This photo "I hope for us to come home together" was taken at a meeting I facilitated in Bratislava in 2013 merging two regional teams. A participant created this sticky note in response to being asked what she most hoped for from our time together. I heard it as a plea from the heart of humanity. I still do.

66   The time it took George Floyd to suffocate under the knee of a police officer in Minneapolis, Minnesota, USA on May 25, 2020.

67   I am indebted to Malaysian academic and activist Dr. Kia Soong Kua for sitting with me to uncover the power of this character.

68   I first described this in Week 31.

69   Find out more about Theory U and Otto Scharmer's work through the Presencing Institute: https://www.presencing.org

70   Michael Ende made just this point in his wonderful book *The Neverending Story*, Thienemann, 1979.

ILLUSTRATIONS

WELCOME TO *365 ALIVE!*
Juskteez Vu @juskteez on Unsplash
Nathan Dumlao @nate_dumlao on Unsplash
Nathan Dumlao @nate_dumlao on Unsplash
Josh Mills @jkmills on Unsplash
Hugh Han @hughhan on Unsplash
Mesh @crypticsy on Unsplash

PART ONE: GETTING STARTED WITH STORY
Rod Long @rodlong on Unsplash
Week 1: Inbetween Architects @inbetween on Unsplash
Week 2: kt lung @ktlung on Unsplash
Week 3: Tim Marshall @timmarshall on Unsplash
Week 4: Drew Taylor @replicantman on Unsplash

PART TWO: MAPPING YOUR PERSONAL STORYFIELD
Jay Wennington @jaywennington on Unsplash
Week 5: Kirsty Barnby @kirstybarnby on Unsplash
Week 6: Erin Song @erindesong on Unsplash
Week 7: Rene Bernal @renebbernal on Unsplash
Week 8: Annie Spratt @anniespratt on Unsplash
Week 9: Author's own
Week 10: Nathália Rosa @nathaliarosa on Unsplash
Week 11: Jaredd Craig @jaredd_craig on Unsplash
Week 12: Author's own
Week 13: Blake Cheek @blakecheekk on Unsplash
Week 14: Jeremy Bishop @jeremybishop on Unsplash
Week 15: James Pond @jamesponddotco on Unsplash
Week 16: Elias Maurer @snowidesinz on Unsplash
Week 17: Tammy Gan @tammynaz on Unsplash
Week 18: Hunter Brummels @hbrumels on Unsplash
Week 19: Ewa Pinkonhead @pinkonhead on Unsplash
Week 20: Sourced from Canva.com

Week 21: Joshua Earle @joshuaearle on Unsplash

Week 22: Prateek Gautam @pgauti on Unsplash

Week 23: Sonder Quest @sonderquest on Unsplash

Week 24: Casey Horner @mischevious_penguins on Unsplash

Week 25: James Sutton @jamessutton_photography on Unsplash

Week 26: Sourced from Canva.com

Week 27: Sourced from Canva.com

Week 28: Markus Spiske @markusspiske on Unsplash

PART THREE: STORY AT WORK IN THE WORLD

Nathan Anderson @nathananderson on Unsplash

Week 29: Sourced from Canva.com

Week 30: Sander Dalhuisen @sanderdalhuisen on Unsplash

Week 31: Jordan Whitt @jwwhitt on Unsplash

Week 32: Author's own

Week 33: Author's own

Week 34: James Behesti @jb2018 on Unsplash

Week 35: Stefano Pollio @stefanopollio on Unsplash

Week 36: Oscar Keys @oscartothekeys on Unsplash

Week 37: Daniel Mayovskiy @godje on Unsplash

Week 38: Robson Hatukami Morgan @robsonhmorgan on Unsplash

Week 39: Sourced from Canva.com

Week 40: Sourced from Canva.com

Week 41: Josh Felise @jfelise on Unsplash

Week 42: James Owen @jhjowen on Unsplash

Week 43: Patrick Fore @patrickian4 on Unsplash

PART FOUR: YOUR FUTURE STORY

Nine Köpfer @enka80 on Unsplash

Week 44: Author's own

Week 45: Author's own

Week 46: Michelle Cassar @cassar_photography on Unsplash

Week 47: Joshua Sortino @sortino on Unsplash

Week 48: Tim Mossholder @timmossholder on Unsplash

Week 49: Sourced from Canva.com

Week 50: Sourced from Canva.com

Week 51: Luke Stackpoole @withluke on Unsplash

Week 52: Sourced from Canva.com

REMEMBER — YOUR STORY MATTERS!

Tom Gainor @its_tgain on Unsplash

EPILOGUE

Jonny Caspari on Unsplash

Author's own

Chinese character Ting

Paul Schafer @paulschafer on Unsplash

Nitin Shah @hope1234 on Unsplash

GRATITUDE

Annie Spratt @anniespratt on Unsplash

BIO

Sandra Seitamaa @sietamaaphotography on Unsplash

Author photo: Author's own

REVIEW

Markus Winkler @markuswinkler on Unsplash

Gratitude is not a big enough word for the joy and learning I've found through working with story. It calls to the deepest part of our humanity and offers a wake-up call to what we think we are and what we dream we can be.

THANK YOU to all of you who have been participants and co-creators in my work through the years, especially all of you who have held a mirror to my work and life and asked me to see the beauty and potential you saw. To my STORY THE FUTURE co-hosts Amy Lenzo, David Hutchens and David Drake, it has been a blessing to sit at the long-time fireside with you and share windows into the soul of humanity. To the STORY THE FUTURE community, gratitude for stoking the fire and believing in the many facets of story. To the BEYOND STORYTELLING team and community, especially Chené Swart, thanks for calling me to craft and share what I know. To the ART OF HOSTING community, especially Monica Níssen and Toke Paludan Møller, co-birthers of the *Collective Story Harvest* process and Ria Baeck, Kajsa Balkfors, Penny Hamilton, Lina Cramer, Yurie Makihara, Samantha Slade, Paul Messer and all of you who have asked me to bring this work to your place. To Helle Solvang and Nadja Pass who have kept the flame of the Denmark 1813 story alive. To the founding team and community of the GOLDEN FLEECE, especially Madelyn Blair and Paul Costello, thank you for creating the beginning place for storytelling in organizations. Thank you to Juanita Brown for encouraging me to see the gifts in this work and for walking the path to embracing story as part of hers. Thank you to Peter Block, for reminding me that writing is a choice and gifting on the treasures I'm holding is a mighty reason. To Sarah Arthur Ronayne for her sisterly support and artistic eye. And finally, thank you to Liz Miller, Moira Wairama, Tony Hopkins, Ralph Johnson, the Glistening Waters team, all who have told and listened at the Wellington Storytellers Café, and Aotearoa herself for opening the door to story for me. *Aroha atu. Aroha mai.*

A bow of gratitude to Avril Orloff for applying her skills and fine eye to the design of this book and the *365 ALIVE!* project. A big THANK YOU to Elizabeth Flannery and Suzanne Thackston for their skillful editing and ongoing encouragement. Huge thanks to Anne Champagne of Green Words Writing and Editing for her very thorough copy editing. And appreciation to all the skilled photographers of Unsplash.com for the way they help us to see beauty in this world.

INDEX

Note: Bold page numbers refer to illustrations

A

Agency, 2, 41, 94, 98, 157, 170, 179, 180, 234, 253
American Sign Language, 145
Appreciation, 13, 214, 261
As It Is in Heaven, 239, 256
Assumptions, 163, 202
Atlee, Tom, 253
Attention, 5, 20, 21, 51, 65, 66, 74, 78, 86, 95, 107, 115, 133, 135–137, 144, 145, 157, 163, 166, 175, 183–185, 187, 189, 203, 229, 230, 237–239, 241, 246, 249, 250
    in Take Action exercise, 20, 74, 90, 162–163, 176
Awareness, 5, 13, 21, 63, 98, 184, 213, 246
Axladitsa-Avatakia, 253

B

Baldwin, Christina, 7, 254
Bareilles, Sarah, 256
Berry, Wendell, **120**
Belonging, 140, 179, 201
Bhagavad Gita, 124
Bias, 189
Bitter Greens, **236**
Block, Francesca Lia, **164**
Bolte Taylor, Jill, 42, 253
Borax, Mark, **116**
Brailsford, Barry, 194, 255
"Brave" (Bareilles), 235, 256
Breath and breathing, 65–67, 86, 118, 121, 132, 185, 226, 254
Breathe (Vranich), 67, 254
Brown, Brené, 190
Buddha, **96**
"Bubble travel", 187, 189
Bzeek, Mohamed, 149

C

Campbell, Joseph, **108, 208, 212,** 213
Categorizing, 127, 203
Challenges, iii, iv, v, 2, 10, 13, 19, 21, 37, 53, 54, 77, 78, 85, 102, 105, 106, 109, 111, 140, 161, 162, 180, 209, 213, 214
Childhood, 1, 35, 46, 53, 131, 157, 199, 238, 239
Cider with Rosie, 53, 254
Cities, ii, 21
Collage, 230
Commitment, 6, 8, 16, 221, 222, 241
Community, v, 19, 23, 25, 26, 39, 41, 45, 46, 62, 69, 125, 137, 139, 140, 143, 147, 152, 163, 167, 170, 179, 181, 183, 185, 194, 198, 202, 203, 207, 243, 253, 255, 261, 266, 268
Confusion, 69, 70, 121, 143, 161, 251
Control, 25, 30, 57, 66, 99, 161, 162, 203, 251, 256
Copenhagen, 151
Corrigan, Kelly, **228**
Corrymeela, 204, 255
Courage, ii, 6, 17, 54, 55, 66, 77, 86, 101, 109, 110, 111, 152, 155, 175, 198, 207, 221, 225, 234, 242, 252
COVID-19, iv, 248

Crow and Weasel (Lopez), 255
Csikszentmihalyi, Mihaly, 256
Culture, 2, 26, 27, 30, 31, 42, 62, 122, 135, 148, 165, 171, 188, 193, 234, 253
Curiosity, 8, 10, 13, 15, 16, 65, 66, 136, 157, 167, 194, 241, 246, 249
    as a starting point, 15–17

D

Davis, Donald, **100**
Discomfort, 37
Diversity, 25, 189, 266
Dobrowolski, Patti, 256
Drawing, 110, 231
Dreams, 19, 97, 158, 171, 172, 184, 229
Driver, Adam, 71, 254

E

Eat, Pray, Love (Gilbert), 89, 199, 255
Eisenstein, Charles, 215, 254, 256
Elizondo, Hector, 47, 253
Elliot, Walter, 220
Empathy, 87, 147, 187–190, 246
Ende, Michael, 46, 145, 194, 255, 257
Entelechy, 93
Epitaph, 99
Eulogy, 99
Evolution, i, iii, 63, 248, 250, 252

F

Failure, 2, 54, 97, 221, 237
Fairytale, 36–38, 39, 98, 131, 219
    exercise, 36–38

Family, i, 2, 9, 10, 29, 30, 31, 41, 46, 49, 50, 53, 54, 55, 63, 66, 67, 74, 78, 86, 139, 140, 152, 155, 163, 165, 170, 171, 176, 194, 198, 218, 229, 234, 246, 248, 266
Figure eight, 245
First Nation, 188
Fitzgerald, F. Scott, 188
Flow, 6, 36, 61, 107, 162, 210, 256
Floyd, George, iv, 257
Forsyth, Kate, **236**
Fowler, Karen Joy, **48**
Fractal, 132, 238
Frankl, Viktor, 98, 225, 256
Franklin, Benjamin, 98, 99
Free Listening Movement, 167

G

"Gabriella's Song", 239, 256
Gaiman, Neil, **150**
Geddes, John, **40**
Genius, 221
Gilbert, Elizabeth, **14**, 199, 221, 255, 256
Godard, Jean-Luc, **60**
Grand Canyon, 35, 176
Gratitude, 214, 260, 261
"The Greatest Showman", 219, 256

H

Habits, 42, 189, 204, 226, 248
Hamburg, Germany, 73, 90
Happiness, 153, 255
Harry Potter (series), 46, 55, 78, 195, 255

Harvey, Mandy, 95, 254
Healing, 67, 158, 165, 175, 183–185
Heroes, 17, 70, 81, 82, 114, 163
Hill, Napoleon, **126**
Holman, Peggy, 253
Honesty, 89–91, 132, 184
Houston, Jean, **112, **114, **178**

I

Identity, i, 33, 78, 79, 122, 140, 156
Images, 1, 27, 61
Imagination, 16, 50, 51, 65, 73, 89, 94, 102, 147, 151, 210, 229, 230, 251, 266
Imperfection, 77, 78, 79
"Inclusion Starts With I", 141, 255
Inner critic, 42, 43, 131
Inspiration, 1, 70, 137, 222
    from childhood books, 45
    from heroes, 70
Intuition, 6, 36, 199, 213, 214

J

James, William, **244**
Japan, 163, 184, 193, 197, 241
Jiwa, Bernadette, **138**
Jones, James Earl, 47, 253

K

Kahn, Matt, **68**
Kahane, Adam, 181, 255
Kendall-Taylor, Nat, 22, 253
King, Dr. Martin Luther, Jr., 181, 233
Kirby, Matthew J., **232**

L

Lancewood, Miriam and Peter, 27
Leadership, i, 98, 106, 210, 215, 233
Lee, Laurie, **52,** 53, 254
The Last Word, 99
Listening, 6, 26, 37, 46, 135, 136, 141, 144, 145, 148, 152, 153, 158, 161, 166, 167, 183, 184, 185, 190, 194, 198, 250, 255
    as Take Action technique, 144–145, 152–153, 158, 166–167
The Little Prince, 129
"Logotherapy", 226
The Lord of the Rings, 119, 194, 223, 255
Lorenzana, Ashly, **56, 84, 104, 154**
Lopez, Barry, **196,** 255
Love, iv, 1, 9, 10, 17, 43, 45, 47, 50, 53, 67, 73, 77, 81, 86, 89, 93, 114, 118, 129, 143, 144, 145, 162, 169, 175, 177, 179, 181, 194, 195, 198, 199, 210, 211, 218, 219, 222, 229, 230, 233, 234, 238, 241, 246, 247, 250, 253, 255, 256, 261, 266, 267

M

Maguire, Gregory, **44**
Maira, Arun, 124, 254
Man's Search for Meaning, 226, 256
Map, 15, 33, 69, 70, 78, 79, 122, 128, 194, 195, 204, 218, 253, 258
    as Take Action technique, 78–79, 218

McCullough, David, Jr., **34**
McHugh, Caroline, 254
Meade, Michael, **247**
Meaning, iii, 2, 5, 13, 20, 21, 33, 41, 49, 58, 78, 79, 94, 113, 114, 115, 139, 140, 141, 152, 153, 156, 157, 170, 180, 183, 194, 198, 226, 227, 237, 238, 250, 251, 252, 256
Memories, i, 29, 33, 49, 50, 51, 53–55, 131, 180, 198
    shaped by story, 29, 33, 49–51
    reliving, 50, 53–55, 198
    using story to define, 29, 33, 49, 57–59
Mentor, 16, 46, 114, 115
Messiness, 143, 144
Miller, Donald, **80**
Millman, Dan, **240**
Mindfulness, 122, 185
Mirror, ii, 5, 7, 10, 67, 123, 184, 207, 242, 261
Momo (Ende), 46, 145, 194, 255
Monk Kidd, Sue, **168, 186**
Montezuma's Well, 128
The More Beautiful World Our Hearts Know Is Possible (Eisenstein), 215, 256
Morgenstern, Erin, **192**
Motivation, 58, 77
Movement, i, 27, 66, 73–75, 117–119, 128, 167, 223
Myth, 36, 113–115, 170, 241
Mythic field, 113–115

N

Narrative, see Story
The Neverending Story, 251, 257
New Zealand, 1, 58, 61, 114, 152, 194, 201, 214, 223, 227, 247, 256, 266, 267
Ngozi Adichie, Chimamanda, 31, 253
Nineteen Paper Cranes, 163, 255
Not-knowing, iv, 69–71, 121–122, 132, 213–214, 251
Nye, Bill, 133, 254

O

Observation (Also see Attention), ii, 51, 162
    of detail, 51
The Odyssey, 114
Okri, Ben, **24**
Opportunity, iv, 5, 8, 114, 121, 127, 128, 132, 144, 187, 238
Oral storytelling, 1
Ordinary People, 67, 133
Oxytocin, 147, 179

P

Pain, 85–87, 132, 184, 188, 190
Parenting, 20
"People on the Move", 255
Perseverance, 221–223
Perspective, 5, 6, 8, 30, 33, 35–38, 43, 46, 50, 63, 113, 119, 122, 129, 145, 151–153, 158, 238
Play, 37, 41, 42, 54, 58, 62, 67, 81,

89, 140, 151, 155, 156, 223, 249
Posey, A.D., **142**
Possibilities, iii, iv, 25, 31, 93, 118, 123, 179–181, 183, 185, 194, 195
Potential, 2, 8, 31, 93–95, 123, 128, 132, 156, 157, 166, 176, 209, 261, 267
Power, i, iii, iv, 2, 29, 38, 42, 98, 109, 118, 119, 123, 132, 136, 140, 147, 148, 152, 156, 161–163, 179, 180, 181, 184, 188, 217, 219, 226, 227, 233–235, 237–239, 245, 250, 254 255, 257, 266, 267
Power and Love: A Theory and Practice of Social Change (Kahane), 181, 255
Practice, 6, 7, 8, 10, 70, 73, 97, 102, 103, 107, 109, 111, 133, 153, 155, 156, 157, 185, 189, 198, 199, 207, 222, 234, 241, 246, 250, 253, 254, 255, 266, 267
Principles, 222
Propaganda, 29
Purpose, 78, 109, 115, 123, 139, 153, 170, 179, 180, 181, 183, 194, 210, 214, 225, 245, 266

Q

Question, iv, 7, 43, 82, 101, 121–124, 144, 149, 180, 181, 201, 202, 254
as Take Action technique, 180–181

R

Rabbit-Proof Fence, 172
Ready Player One, 103, 254
Reid, Vanessa, 253
The Rescued Film Project, 51, 254
Resilience, 54, 55, 73, 155–158, 246
Resistance, 8, 37, 122, 226
The Return of the King (Tolkien), 223, 256
Rowling, J.K., 55, 254, 255
Rushdie, Salman, **160**
Russell, Keri, **224**

S

Sagan, Carl, **174**, 175, 255
Scanlon, Dan, **72**
Scordialos, Maria, 253, 255
Scars, 156
Scharmer, Otto, 250
"Seasons of Love", 211, 256
Secrets, 170, 171, 249
Seeds, iv, 94, 131–133, 242
Senses, 27, 36, 50, 103, 135, 151–153
function in story, 49–51, 151
Shah, Tahir, **18**
Shaw, Martin, 3
A Single Life, 63, 254
Slowing down, 127–129, 185
Social media, 30, 85, 101, 157, 184, 202, 203
Solomon, Andrew, 79, 254
Song of Waitaha, 255
Stamina, 73, 109, 198, 207, 221–223
Star Wars, 114
"Start Close In" (Whyte), 234, 256
Story
archaeologist of, 26
as architecture of memory, 29–31, 49–51, 57–59
attention to, 19–22, 183–185
breath, importance of, 65–67
changing, 201–204
cultural shaping of, 41–43
de-storying and re-storying, **164**, 165–167, 170
"fish stories", 89–91
hidden, 110, 169–172, 179–181, 204, 217, 252
in environment, 19–22, 25, 75
in families, 2, 4, 9, 10, 29–31, 41, 46, 49, 50, 53, 54, 55, 63, 66, 67, 152, 163, 165, 170, 171, 194, 198, 246, 248
health of, 13, 25–27
holding in trust, 197–199
impact of, iv, 2, 26, 87, 91, 98, 193–195, 207, 225–227
intention of, 19–22
meaning of: as a human practice of making meaning through stories, iii, 2, 20, 33, 58, 79, 113, 114, 139, 140, 152, 156, 170, 180, 183, 194, 198, 226, 227, 251, 252; as a personal practice of making meaning through stories: 2, 5, 13, 20, 21, 41, 49, 78, 79, 94, 115, 139, 140, 153, 157, 237, 238
movement in, 73–75, 117–119
power of, i, iii, iv, 2, 29, 132, 136, 161–163, 184, 237, 245, 250, 254, 266
presence for, 155–158, 165–167, 183–185

reclaiming, 165–167, 171, 234
responsibility for, 201–204
rewriting, 73–75, 77–79, 81–83
senses, 49–51, 103
shaping, iii, 13, 41–43, 49–51, 61–63, 97–99, 105–107, 245
"stuck" places in, 3, 31, 36, 46, 49, 66, 67, 69–71, 73–75, 77–79, 117–119, 122, 132, 144, 165, 203, 204, 226, 238
truth of, 89–91, 113
unheard, see hidden
waking up to, 2, 13, 61–63
way shower, 193–195
Story Activism, i, 2–3, 136, 151–153, 207, 267
   definition, 2–3, 136, 153
StoryCatcher, 139–141, 209–211, 254, 267
StoryField, 33, 61–63, 165–167, 201–204, 246, 253, 258
   conference, 253
   definition, 6, 165, 246, 253
Storymaking, 241–242, 246
Story Roles
   Story Activist 2, 3, 136, 153, 207
   StoryCatcher 141, 210, 267
   Storyteller, 1, 2, 13, 15, 50, 66, 110, 132, 141, 144, 145, 147, 161, 198, 245, 266
Storyteller, 1, 2, 13, 15–17, 19–22, 49–51, 65–67, 101–103, 109–111, 131–163, 169–172, 197–199, 245, 255, 266, 267
StoryWork, 6, 131–133, 267
Studio Ghibli, 177
Success, 2, 10, 70, 90, 124, 201–204, 221–223
Such Is Life, 185, 255
Suffering, 85, 170, 190, 221, 225–227
Superpower, 207, 217–219
Surrender, 213–215, 250
Survival, 30

T

Team, 15, 16, 69, 86, 90, 149, 152, 209, 261
   setting up your journey, 15–17
Telling your story, 49, 59, 81–83, 90, 118, 152, 158, 170, 202, 204, 205, 239, 250
   as Take Action exercise, 152–153
The Thirteenth Floor, 103
"This Is Me", 256
Thordis, Elva, and Stranger, Tom, 255
Tolkien, J.R.R., 194, 255
Touching, 165–167, 177
Transformation, 77, 238
Trauma, 86, 237, 238, 249
Travel, 10, 19–22, 30, 73, 102, 133, 187, 189, 214, 229, 247
Tree, 93–95, 121
   as identity, 93–95
   as metaphor, 93–95
Truth, 49, 89–91, 113, 207
Twain, Mark, **88,** 89

U

Umbrella Academy, 86

V

Vision board, see Collage
Vocation, 123
Vranich, Belisa, 67, 254

W

Waldinger, Robert, 255
Walker, Alice, **182**
Waking up (as a function of story), 2, 13
Warner, Marina, **146**
Way shower, see Stories, way shower
Whiteley, Sarah, 253
Whitmore, John, 92
Whyte, David, 234, 256
Witnessing/with-nessing, 147–149, 155, 156, 162, 250
Wonder, sense of, 175–177, 210, 242
Wong, Emily, 185, 255
Worman, Troy, **76**
Wounding, 86, 95, 155–158, 171, 172
Wright, Jeffrey, 43, 253

Z

Zusya, Rabbi, 94

Here's the story

I got hooked on stories from the first moment I saw a book. I was the kid who kept reading after lights out and walked to school reading two books at once (fortunately, I grew up in a flat place!). I now look back and realize that my first travels were journeys of the imagination. During school holidays the family piled into the car and took to the roads, and that gave me an itchy foot. Before long I was seventeen. Becoming an exchange student gave me my first taste of the wider world. By the time I was nineteen I had enough fluency in another language to study abroad and work as a translator. This experience gave me a somatic sense of the power of language. The stage was set for a love of wondering coupled with a delight in wandering — the ideal attributes for a storyteller and a self-professed citizen of the world.

Working with an international student organization during my university years taught me the power of passion and the strength that comes from working across diversity. I learned about the compelling nature of purpose, the importance of a spark of vision and the power of cohesive practice. I began to think — and work — around the world.

I caught the story bug in earnest while living in New Zealand. It happened at the 1992 Glistening Waters, the first international storytelling festival. That was the moment when I saw the power of storytelling for the first time. I started hanging out in the library gathering as many stories as I could. I still remember another storyteller telling me she told "stories that fit on my tongue" and learned how accurate that was as a measure for choosing which stories to tell. I performed as a storyteller, but I soon realized I wanted to hear others voices more than just my own. There seemed to be something important in sharing stories and working with them. That's why I was part of the first gatherings of organizational storytelling practitioners a decade later.

At the same time I was honing my craft as a facilitator, working with everyone from the Treasury and government departments to volunteer organizations. I worked to connect teams, support groups to get strategic, I even facilitated a successful telecommunications merger. In 2007 I found out about the Art of Hosting community

> **Life is all about the stories we tell and how we bring them alive.**

and began to more strongly integrate my work as a practitioner. Then I met a futurist at a conference who told me one of the top upcoming trends would be "leader as storyteller" and I began to dream of the day my process work and my love of stories would unite.

One day, I watched a short interview with New Zealand actor Cliff Curtis as he talked about how good stories make you want to take action, get committed, do something. *That's it*, I thought, I'm a *Story Activist!* The journey since then has been a discovery of how story and hosting blend to help change arise, compelling stories be created and people to work together.

After almost thirty years in New Zealand, I spent more than five years on the road with no fixed address. I called myself an intentional nomad, and I defined that as moving between people and places to witness and enliven them. I found myself picking up stories in one place and taking them to the next place that needed them. It has been an excellent training as a StoryCatcher and storyteller.

Find and share STORIES of us at our best as a humanity.

Let them FLY and see what we grow together.

— MARY ALICE ARTHUR

Now I join StoryWork with a leading-edge skill in using participatory practice to help groups become high-performing communities, able to step up, co-create a compelling story, and from it, wise sustained action. I've worked around the world with leaders in all levels of public and private organizations and communities. As an international steward of the Art of Hosting network, I teach StoryWorking skills and participatory practice, and host participatory gatherings all over the globe.

While storytelling has always been an art and a skill that is lived face-to-face and practiced heart to heart, I am incredibly heartened to know that it also flourishes online, bringing us closer, no matter where we happen to be.

Here's the serious stuff

Mary Alice Arthur is a Story Activist, using story to create positive systemic shift and for applying collective intelligence to the critical issues of our times. Her art is in creating brave and transformational spaces where people can find their most compelling stories and develop the practices to live into them. Joining StoryWork and participatory practice means people can make wiser choices together. She is a sought-after process consultant and a favorite at events. In her client and coaching work people develop the skills and practice to engage others in leading-edge conversations about the power and potential in our world.

Connect with Mary Alice

Web: www.getsoaring.com Explore the website and see other offerings and products that can help you take this work deeper. Subscribe to my newsletter and get the latest information on story and how you can expand your skills.

LinkedIn: www.linkedin.com/in/mary-alice-arthur/

Twitter: @StoryActivist

Facebook: https://www.facebook.com/getsoaring

Instagram: http://instagram.com/maryalicearthur

365 ALIVE! Resources

Visit www.365alive.org and find additional resources to support your story journey, including the *365 ALIVE!* card deck, opportunities to meet with the *365 ALIVE!* Community and more.

Thank you for taking the *365 ALIVE!* Journey

What have you learned along the way that could benefit other readers or help me to make either this book, or the support materials around it, even more awesome?

Please help this book come into the hands of readers around the world by leaving a helpful review on Amazon.

Thanks so much & happy story sharing!

Mary Alice

www.ingramcontent.com/pod-product-compliance
Lightning Source LLC
Chambersburg PA
CBHW051255110526
44589CB00025B/2839